W9-CTC-673

College Reading Skills

Selections from the Black, Book Two
Provocative Selections by Black Writers
Third Edition

Edward Spargo, Editor

Consultant for Editorial Content:
Barry Beckham
Associate Professor of English
Brown University

Consultant for Instructional Design:
Mary Prosser Rynn
Staff Developer
New York City Public Schools

Books in the Series:
Book One   Book Three
Book Two   Book Four

Jamestown Publishers

Selections from the Black, Book Two

Third Edition

Catalog No. 822
© 1989 by Jamestown Publishers, Inc.

Cover and text design by Deborah Hulsey Christie

Cover credit: 1974.41. *Ubi Girl from Tai Region.* Lois Jones. Oil on acrylic. 110 × 150 cm. Charles Henry Hayden Collection. Courtesy, Museum of Fine Arts, Boston

Picture Credits: Schomburg Center, N.Y.P.L.: Lois M. Jones; Robert Allen: Alice Walker; Helen Marcus: Toni Morrison; Mary Ellen Mark: Maya Angelou; Moorland-Spingarn Research Center, Howard University: Frederick Douglass, Langston Hughes, Booker T. Washington, Malcolm X; Reuters/Bettmann Newsphotos: H. Rap Brown; Mario Ruiz: Wallace Terry; University of Wyoming: John Edgar Wideman

Printed in the United States of America
5   6   7   8   PO   98   97

ISBN: 0-89061-483-0

Readability			
Book One	F–G	Book Three	J–K
Book Two	H–I	Book Four	L–up

Acknowledgments

Acknowledgment is gratefully made to the following publishers and authors for permission to reprint excerpts from these works.

Go Tell It on the Mountain. Text excerpt from *Go Tell It on the Mountain* by James Baldwin. Copyright © 1952, 1953 by James Baldwin. Reprinted by permission of The Dial Press, Inc.

'Tain't So. From *The Book of Negro Humor* edited by Langston Hughes. Reprinted by permission of Dodd, Mead & Company.

Jubilee. Text excerpt from *Jubilee* by Margaret Walker. Copyright © 1966 by Margaret Walker Alexander. Reprinted by permission of Houghton Mifflin Company.

Up From Slavery. Excerpt from *Up From Slavery* by Booker T. Washington. (1900)

Die, Nigger, Die. Text excerpt from *Die, Nigger, Die* by H. Rap Brown. Copyright © 1969 by Lynne Brown. Reprinted by permission of The Dial Press, Inc.

What to the Slaves Is the Fourth of July? Excerpt from Frederick Douglass's Independence Day Address, 1852.

The Autobiography of Malcolm X. Text excerpt from *The Autobiography of Malcolm X* by Malcolm X. Copyright © 1965 by Alex Haley and Betty Shabazz. Reprinted by permission of Grove Press, Inc.

The Color Purple. Text excerpt from *The Color Purple* by Alice Walker. Copyright © 1982 by Alice Walker. Reprinted by permission of Harcourt Brace Jovanovich, Inc.

Sula, I, II. Text excerpts from *Sula* by Toni Morrison. Copyright © 1973 by Toni Morrison. Reprinted by permission of Random House, Inc.

The Heart of a Woman. Text excerpt from *The Heart of a Woman* by Maya Angelou. Copyright © 1981 by Maya Angelou. Reprinted by permission of Random House, Inc.

Anticipation. From *An African Treasury,* edited by Langston Hughes. Reprinted by permission of Mabel Dove-Danquah.

Contents

1 | Introductory Selection

*Explains How the Text is Organized and
How to Use It to Maximum Advantage*

Vocabulary—The five words below are from the story you are about to read.
Study the words and their meanings. Then complete the ten sentences that
follow, using one of the five words to fill in the blank in each sentence.
Mark your answer by writing the letter of the word on the line before the
sentence. Check your answers in the Answer Key on page 106.

A. intent: purpose

B. moderate: calm; avoiding extremes

C. servitude: lack of freedom; slavery

D. corresponding: matching

E. efficient: performing a task easily and skillfully

_____ 1. Some of the selections describe the conditions endured by blacks
who lived a life of _____ .

_____ 2. The demands of some black leaders have been extreme; the
demands of others have been _____ .

_____ 3. As you work through each selection, you will become more
_____ at analyzing written material.

_____ 4. After finishing the book, you will have a good grasp of its
_____ .

_____ 5. The skilled reader has learned that each kind of reading matter
demands a _____ reading technique.

_____ 6. Some people predicted the book would lead to further separation
of the races, but more _____ voices welcomed the book.

_____ 7. In order to be an _____ reader, you must sharpen your critical
reading skills.

_____ 8. To communicate with their readers is the _____ of all authors.

_____ 9. Writers, both moderate and extreme, make their arguments in language _____ to their views.

_____ 10. Some of the selections will help you understand the history and
background of black people's _____ .

(Before you begin reading this selection, turn to page 8 and record the hours and minutes in the box labeled *Starting Time* at the bottom of the second column. If you are using this text in class and your instructor has made provisions for timing, you need not stop now; read on.)

You are using this text for two purposes: (1) to improve your reading and study skills, (2) to read what black people are saying now and what they have said in the past.

Twenty years ago, when *Selections from the Black* was first published, our nation was just beginning to realize that blacks had a voice and had something to say. Jamestown's intent was to assemble these writings and publish them so that our texts might racially balance the other literature college students were expected to read. When these texts were first published, there were objections from those who felt that a menu of exclusively black writings only served to further isolate blacks from the American mainstream.

Fortunately, moderate thought prevailed, and the concept of a black reading and study skills program was accepted. In the intervening years tens of thousands of students, black and white, have used *Selections from the Black* with satisfaction and success.

In the selections that follow you will read the words of slaves describing their days of oppression. You will read the words of yesterday's leaders—DuBois, Garvey, Washington and others—and begin to understand the history and background of Negro servitude. You will understand how their thinking influenced their times and ours.

You will read the words of those from the more recent past describing the explosive racial climate of the 1950s and 1960s. This text presents the voices of protest, moderate and defiant, including those silenced by death, exile, and imprisonment. Writers of both extremes are presented here because their words have structured and defined black America.

You will also read the words of people who live under, and struggle against, South Africa's white-minority rule and policy of apartheid. Their messages are important to us because apartheid has become an issue of international proportions.

Black men and women writing about politics, sports, business, journalism, and entertainment have contributed to these selections. Also included are many master writers of fiction; their stories, rich with feeling, are part of the treasury of black literature.

We want you to enjoy these selections, and we want you to learn from them. We especially want you to understand the situation of the black person over time and throughout history.

The other purpose for using this text, that of reading and study improvement, recognizes reality, too: the reality

"It is important to understand the situation of the black person over time and throughout history."

of today. This text will help you to develop skills and techniques necessary for efficiency in our society.

Included in each selection are two Study Skills exercises. In these, you will learn methods of understanding, critical thinking skills, techniques of comprehension, and many other key ways to improve your reading ability. Both Study Skill exercises are designed to assist you in developing efficient reading techniques. As you read the selections in this book, you will find that often one Study Skills exercise leads directly to the next. It is important to read and work the Study Skills exercises consecutively in order to understand fully each subject.

Today's reader must be flexible enough to choose from a supply of skills one that is suitable for each reading task. The skilled reader has learned that each kind of reading matter demands a corresponding reading technique— there is no single "best" way to read. As you complete the selections and exercises in this book, you will find yourself growing in technique.

Using the Text

The twenty selections are designed to be read in numerical order, starting with the Introductory Selection and ending with Selection 20. Because the selections increase in difficulty as you progress through the book, the earlier ones prepare you to handle successfully the upcoming ones.

Here are the procedures to follow for reading each selection.

1. Answer the Vocabulary Questions. Immediately preceding each selection is a vocabulary previewing exercise. The exercise includes five vocabulary words from the selection, their meanings, and ten fill-in-the-blank sentences. To complete each sentence you will fill in the blank with one of the five vocabulary words.

Previewing the vocabulary in such a fashion will give you a head start on understanding the words when you encounter them in the selection. The fill-in-the-blank sentences present each word in context (surrounding words). That provides you with the chance to improve your ability to use context as an aid in understanding words. The efficient use of context is a valuable vocabulary tool.

After you have filled in the blanks in all ten sentences, check your answers in the Answer Key that starts on page 106. Be sure you understand the correct meaning of any wrong answers.

2. Preview before Reading. Previewing acquaints you with the overall content and structure of the selection before you actually read. It is like consulting a road map before taking a trip: planning the route gives you more confidence as you proceed and, perhaps, helps you avoid any unnecessary delays. Previewing should take about a minute or two and is done in this way:

a) Read the Title. Learn the writer's subject and, possibly, his point of view on it.

b) Read the Opening and Closing Paragraphs. These contain the introductory and concluding remarks. Important information is frequently presented in these key paragraphs.

c) Skim through. Try to discover the author's approach to his subject. Does he use many examples? Is his purpose to sell you his ideas? What else can you learn now to help you when you read?

3. Read the Selection. Do not try to race through. Read well and carefully enough so that you can answer the comprehension questions that follow.

Keep track of your reading time by noting when you start and finish. A table on page 110 converts your reading time to a words-per-minute rate. Select the time from the table that is closest to your reading time. Record those figures in the boxes at the end of the selection. There is no one ideal reading speed for everything. The efficient reader varies his speed as the selection requires.

Many selections include a brief biography and perhaps a photograph of the author. Do not include this in your reading time. It is there to introduce you to the writer. Many of the selections have been reprinted from full-length books and novels. Complete information is contained in a bibliography on page 109. If you find a particular selection interesting, you may enjoy reading the entire book.

4. Answer the Comprehension Questions. After you have read the selection, find the comprehension questions that follow. These have been included to test your understanding of what you have read. The questions are diagnostic, too. Because the comprehension skill being measured is identified, you can detect your areas of weakness.

Read each question carefully and, without looking back, select one of the four choices given that answers that question most accurately or most completely. Frequently all four choices, or options, given for a question are *correct*, but one is the *best* answer. For this reason the comprehension questions are highly challenging and require you to be highly discriminating. You may, from time to time, disagree with the choice given in the Answer Key. When this happens, you have an opportunity to sharpen your powers of discrimination. Study the question again and seek to discover why the listed answer may be best. When you disagree with the text, you are thinking; when you objectively analyze and recognize your errors, you are learning.

The Answer Key begins on page 106. Find the answers for your selection and correct your comprehension work. When you discover a wrong answer, circle it and check the correct one.

The boxes following each selection contain space for your comprehension and vocabulary scores. Each correct vocabulary item is worth ten points and each correct comprehension answer is worth ten points.

Pages 111 and 112 contain graphs to be used for plotting your scores and tallying your incorrect responses. On page 111 record your comprehension score at the appropriate intersection of lines, using an *X*. Use a circle, or some other mark, on the same graph to record your vocabulary results. Some students prefer to use different color inks, or pencil and ink, to distinguish between comprehension and vocabulary plottings.

On page 112 darken in the squares to indicate the comprehension questions you have missed. By referring to the Skills Profile as you progress through the text, you and your instructor will be able to tell which questions give you the most trouble. As soon as you detect a specific weakness in comprehension, consult with your instructor to see what supplementary materials he or she can provide or suggest.

A profitable habit for you to acquire is the practice of analyzing the questions you have answered incorrectly. If time permits, return to the selection to find and underline the passages containing the correct answers. This helps you to see what you missed the first time. Some interpretive and generalization type questions are not answered specifically in the text. In these cases bracket that part of the selection that alludes to the correct answer. Your instructor may recommend that you complete this step outside of class as homework.

5. Complete the Study Skills Exercises. Following the comprehension questions in each chapter is a passage on study skills. Some of the sentences in the passage have blanks where words have been omitted. Next to the passage are groups of five words, one group for each blank. Your task is to complete the passage by selecting the correct word for each of the blanks.

Next are five completion questions to be answered after you have reread the study skills passage.

The same answer key you have been using gives the correct responses for these two study skills exercises.

If class time is at a premium, your instructor may prefer that you complete the exercises out of class.

The following selections in this text are structured just like this introductory one. Having completed this selection and its exercises, you will then be prepared to proceed to Selection 2.

Starting Time		Finishing Time	
Reading Time		Reading Rate	
Comprehension		Vocabulary	

Comprehension— Read the following questions and statements. For each one, put an *x* in the box before the option that contains the most complete or accurate answer. Check your answers in the Answer Key on page 106.

1. How much time should you devote to previewing a selection?
   - ☐ a. Your time will vary with each selection.
   - ☐ b. You should devote about one or two minutes to previewing.
   - ☐ c. No specific time is suggested.
   - ☐ d. None—the instructor times the selection.

2. The way the vocabulary exercises are described suggests that
   - ☐ a. the meaning of a word often depends on how it is used.
   - ☐ b. the final authority for word meaning is the dictionary.
   - ☐ c. words have precise and permanent meanings.
   - ☐ d. certain words are always difficult to understand.

3. The writer of this passage presents the facts in order of
   - ☐ a. importance.
   - ☐ b. purpose.
   - ☐ c. time.
   - ☐ d. operation.

4. *Selections from the Black* is based on which of the following premises?
   - ☐ a. Literature for college students needed to be racially balanced.
   - ☐ b. Black students learn best from black writers.
   - ☐ c. The writings of black authors should provoke student interest.
   - ☐ d. Traditional reading improvement texts are racially unfair.

5. How does the writer feel about reading speed?
   - ☐ a. It is a minimal aspect of the total reading situation.
   - ☐ b. It is second (following comprehension) in the ranking of skills.
   - ☐ c. It is connected to comprehension.
   - ☐ d. It should be developed at an early age.

6. The introductory selection
   - ☐ a. eliminates the need for oral instruction.
   - ☐ b. explains the proper use of the text in detail.
   - ☐ c. permits the student to learn by doing.
   - ☐ d. allows for variety and interest.

7. The introductory selection suggests that
   - ☐ a. most readers are not flexible.
   - ☐ b. students should learn to use different reading skills for different types of reading matter.
   - ☐ c. students today read better than students of the past did.
   - ☐ d. twenty selections is an ideal number for a reading improvement text.

8. The overall tone of this passage is
   - ☐ a. serious.
   - ☐ b. suspenseful.
   - ☐ c. humorous.
   - ☐ d. sarcastic.

9. The author of this selection is probably
   - ☐ a. a doctor.
   - ☐ b. an accountant.
   - ☐ c. an educator.
   - ☐ d. a businessman.

10. The writer of this passage makes his point clear by
   - ☐ a. telling a story.
   - ☐ b. listing historical facts.
   - ☐ c. using metaphors.
   - ☐ d. giving directions.

Comprehension Skills	
1. recalling specific facts	6. making a judgment
2. retaining concepts	7. making an inference
3. organizing facts	8. recognizing tone
4. understanding the main idea	9. understanding characters
5. drawing a conclusion	10. appreciation of literary forms

Study Skills, Part One—Following is a passage with blanks where words have been omitted. Next to the passage are groups of five words, one group for each blank. Complete the passage by circling the correct word for each of the blanks.

Paragraphs of Introduction

The textbook writer works through paragraphs. The ___(1)___ with which he communicates with his readers depends on how well and how carefully he has structured his paragraphs.

(1)   effort   easiness
    importance   efficiency   effectiveness

In each chapter or article, the writer begins with an ___(2)___ paragraph. Like a speaker, the writer offers prefacing remarks to open his discussion of a particular topic or subject.

We have all heard the speaker who tells an ___(3)___ or two to "warm up" listeners before he gets into the talk. Writers have a much more difficult task—they are not face to face with their listeners, and must do more than tell an amusing story to get the readers ready for the presentation. Recognizing this limitation of communication through the printed page, writers strive to create an effective opening with which to introduce their subject to the reader.

The opening paragraph is called the paragraph of introduction—used as a kind of announcement of what is to follow. Frequently the writer will state the purpose he hopes to accomplish in the following paragraphs; he may offer a brief outline of the major ___(4)___ he intends to discuss; he may merely mention one or two of the ideas the reader can expect later in the chapter.

Obviously a paragraph of introduction is packed with ___(5)___ . Because it offers such a preview of what is to come, it is one of the only two paragraphs read when previewing. In magazine articles and similar leisure reading publications, the paragraph of introduction has a special function to perform—it's used frequently as bait to ___(6)___ the reader into the account. The feature writer knows that he must capture the reader's interest and attention with just a few words. The reader can expect any kind of interest-compelling ___(7)___ to be employed for this purpose—it is the skilled writer at his best.

| (2) | introductory | innocent |
| | unusual | ordinary | educational |

| (3) | incident | inference |
| | anecdote | observation | secret |

| (4) | opportunities | barriers |
| | conflicts | concepts | errors |

| (5) | significance | statements |
| | questions | judgment | communication |

| (6) | convince | lure |
| | bore | create | move |

| (7) | indexes | devices |
| | chapters | titles | characters |

Study Skills, Part Two—Read the study skills passage again, paying special attention to the lesson being taught. Then, without looking back at the passage, complete each sentence below by writing in the missing word or words. Check the Answer Key on page 106 for the answers to Study Skills, Part One, and Study Skills, Part Two.

1. The textbook writer depends on carefully structured _____ for effective communication.

2. Recognizing his limits within the _____ , the writer must try to create an effective way to introduce the subject to the reader.

3. The paragraph of introduction is used as a sort of _____ of things to come.

4. When _____ , you should be sure to read the paragraph of introduction.

5. The feature writer must capture the reader's attention with just a few _____ .

2 | Go Tell It on the Mountain

by James Baldwin

Vocabulary—The five words below are from the story you are about to read. Study the words and their meanings. Then complete the ten sentences that follow, using one of the five words to fill in the blank in each sentence. Mark your answer by writing the letter of the word on the line before the sentence. Check your answers in the Answer Key on page 106.

A. hysterical: extremely upset; out of control

B. impulse: a sudden desire

C. removed: apart, not close to

D. malice: a feeling of hatred, spite, ill will

E. unreadable: having no expression, blank

_____ 1. John stood _____ from the confusion for a while before entering the living room.

_____ 2. For a brief second John felt the _____ to run from the fear that welled up inside him.

_____ 3. Elizabeth stood by the injured Roy, her face as _____ as a blank piece of paper.

_____ 4. Florence spoke to her brother in a voice that was stern and bore a slight hint of _____ .

_____ 5. Even though her crib was _____ from the living room, the baby Ruth sensed there was trouble in the house.

_____ 6. Before John entered the building, he paused and wondered what had caused his sister's _____ behavior.

_____ 7. Acting on _____ , John quietly told his baby sister to run away from home.

_____ 8. Elizabeth's concern was masked by an _____ expression.

_____ 9. For one brief second John met his father's cold eyes, seeing in them the _____ the man bore toward him.

_____ 10. Panic seized John's thoughts and drove him forward with _____ swiftness.

As John approached his home again in the late afternoon, he saw little Sarah, her coat unbuttoned, come flying out of the house and run the length of the street away from him into the far drugstore. Instantly, he was frightened; he stopped a moment, staring blankly down the street, wondering what could justify such hysterical haste. It was true that Sarah was full of self-importance, and made any errand she ran seem a matter of life or death; nevertheless, she had been sent on an errand, and with such speed that her mother had not had time to make her button up her coat.

Then he felt weary; if something had really happened it would be very unpleasant upstairs now, and he did not want to face it. But perhaps it was simply that his mother had a headache and had sent Sarah to the store for some aspirin. But if this were true, it meant that he would have to prepare supper, and take care of the children, and be naked under his father's eyes all the evening long. And he began to walk more slowly.

There were some boys standing on the stoop. They watched him as he approached, and he tried not to look at them and to approximate the swagger with which they walked. One of them said, as he mounted the short, stone steps and started into the hall: "Boy, your brother was hurt real bad today."

He looked at them in a kind of dread, not daring to ask for details; and he observed that they, too, looked as though they had been in a battle; something hangdog in their looks suggested that they had been put to flight. Then he looked down, and saw that there was blood at the threshold, and blood splattered on the tile floor of the vestibule. He looked again at the boys, who had not ceased to watch him, and hurried up the stairs.

The door was half open—for Sarah's return, no doubt—and he walked in, making no sound, feeling a confused impulse to flee. There was no one in the kitchen, though the light was burning—the lights were on all through the house. On the kitchen table stood a shopping-bag filled with groceries, and he knew that his Aunt Florence had arrived. The washtub, where his mother had been washing earlier, was still open, and filled the kitchen with a sour smell.

There were drops of blood on the floor here too, and there had been small, smudged coins of blood on the stairs as he walked up.

All this frightened him terribly. He stood in the middle of the kitchen, trying to imagine what had happened, and preparing himself to walk into the living-room, where all the family seemed to be. Roy had been in trouble before, but this new trouble seemed to be the beginning of the fulfillment of a prophecy. He took off his coat, dropping it on a chair, and was about to start into the living-room when he heard Sarah running up the steps.

He waited, and she burst through the door, carrying a clumsy parcel.

Some wounds are calamitous, showy—the whole neighborhood knows about them. Other wounds, like John's, are secrets kept in the heart.

"What happened?" he whispered.

She stared at him in astonishment, and a certain wild joy. He thought again that he really did not like his sister. Catching her breath, she blurted out, triumphantly: "Roy got stabbed with a knife!" and rushed into the living-room.

Roy got stabbed with a knife. Whatever this meant, it was sure that his father would be at his worst tonight. John walked slowly into the living-room.

His father and mother, a small basin of water between them, knelt by the sofa where Roy lay, and his father was washing the blood from Roy's forehead. It seemed that his mother, whose touch was so much more gentle, had been thrust aside by his father, who could not bear to have anyone else touch his wounded son. And now she watched, one hand in the water, the other, in a kind of anguish, at her waist, which was circled still by the improvised apron of the morning. Her face, as she watched, was full of pain and fear, of tension barely supported, and of pity that could scarcely have been expressed had she filled all the world with her weeping. His father muttered sweet, delirious things to Roy, and his hands, when he dipped them again in the basin and wrung out the cloth, were trembling. Aunt Florence, still wearing her hat and carrying her handbag, stood a little removed, looking down at them with a troubled, terrible face.

Then Sarah bounded into the room before him, and his mother looked up, reached out for the package, and saw him. She said nothing, but she looked at him with a strange, quick intentness, almost as though there were a warning on her tongue which at the moment she did not dare to utter. His Aunt Florence looked up, and said: "We been wondering where you was, boy. This bad brother of yours done gone out and got hisself hurt."

But John understood from her tone that the fuss was possibly, a little greater than the danger—Roy was not, after all, going to die. And his heart lifted a little. Then his father turned and looked at him.

"Where you been, boy," he shouted, "all this time? Don't you know you's needed here at home?"

More than his words, his face caused John to stiffen instantly with malice and fear. His father's face was terrible in anger, but now there was more than anger in it. John saw now what he had never seen there before, except in his own vindictive fantasies: a kind of wild, weeping terror that made the face seem younger, and yet at the same time unutterably older and more cruel. And John knew, in the moment his father's eyes swept over him, that he hated John because John was not lying on the sofa where Roy lay. John could scarcely meet his father's eyes, and yet, briefly, he did, saying nothing, feeling in his heart an odd sensation of triumph, and hoping in his heart that Roy, to bring his father low, would die.

His mother had unwrapped the package and was opening

a bottle of peroxide. "Here," she said, "you better wash it with this now." Her voice was calm and dry; she looked at his father briefly, her face unreadable, as she handed him the bottle and the cotton.

"This going to hurt," his father said—in such a different voice, so sad and tender!—turning again to the sofa. "But you just be a little man and hold still; it ain't going to take long."

John watched and listened, hating him. Roy began to moan. Aunt Florence moved to the mantel-piece and put her handbag down near the metal serpent. From the room behind him, John heard the baby begin to whimper.

"John," said his mother, "go and pick her up like a good boy." Her hands, which were not trembling, were still busy: she had opened the bottle of iodine and was cutting up strips of bandage.

John walked into his parents' bedroom and picked up the squalling baby, who was wet. The moment Ruth felt him lift her up she stopped crying and stared at him with a wide-eyed, pathetic stare, as though she knew that there was trouble in the house. John laughed at her so ancient-seeming distress—he was very fond of his baby sister—and whispered in her ear as he started back to the living-room: "Now, you let your big brother tell you something, baby. Just as soon as you's able to stand on your feet, you run away from *this* house, run far away." He did not quite know why he said this, or where he wanted her to run, but it made him feel instantly better.

His father was saying, as John came back into the room: "I'm sure going to be having some questions to ask you in a minute, old lady. I'm going to be wanting to know just how come you let this boy go out and get half killed."

"Oh, no, you ain't," said Aunt Florence. "You ain't going to be starting none of that mess this evening. You know right doggone well that Roy don't never ask *nobody* if he can do *nothing*—he just go right ahead and do like he pleases. Elizabeth sure can't put no ball and chain on him. She got her hands full right here in this house, and it ain't her fault if Roy got a head just as hard as his father's."

"You got a awful lot to say, look like for once you could keep from putting your mouth in my business." He said this without looking at her.

"It ain't my fault," she said, "that you was born a fool, and always done been a fool, and ain't never going to change. I swear to my Father you'd try the patience of Job."

Novelist and essayist James Baldwin was born in 1924 in New York City. The first of nine children, he grew up in Harlem, where his father was a minister. He graduated from high school in 1942 and held many minor jobs—handyman, porter, office boy, elevator operator, factory worker, and dishwasher, among others. When he was twenty-four, Baldwin left the United States for a ten-year stay in Europe. Residing mainly in Paris, he wrote and published his first three books. In 1957 Baldwin returned to the United States. For the last several years he had divided his time between a home in southern France and one in New York City. Baldwin died in November, 1987.

Baldwin's published works include two books of autobiographical essays, a collection of short stories, and four novels dealing with racial strife and homosexuality. He achieved recognition as a playwright for two plays, *Blues for Mister Charlie* and *The Amen Corner*, both of which were performed on Broadway, in Europe, and in the Near East. His stories and essays have appeared in many magazines and essays both here and abroad.

"I done told you before," he said—he had not ceased working over the moaning Roy, and was preparing now to dab the wound with iodine—"that I didn't want you coming in here and using that gutter language in front of my children."

"Don't you worry about my language, brother," she said with spirit, "you better start worrying about your *life*. What these children hear ain't going to do them near as much harm as what they *see*."

"What they *see*," his father muttered, "is a poor man trying to serve the Lord. *That's* my life."

"Then I guarantee *you*," she said, "that they going to do their best to keep it from being *their* life. *You* mark my words."

He turned and looked at her, and intercepted the look that passed between the two women. John's mother, for reasons that were not at all his father's reasons, wanted Aunt Florence to keep still. He looked away, ironically. John watched his mother's mouth tighten bitterly as she dropped her eyes. His father, in silence, began bandaging Roy's forehead.

Starting Time		*Finishing Time*	
Reading Time		*Reading Rate*	
Comprehension		*Vocabulary*	

Comprehension— Read the following questions and statements. For each one, put an *x* in the box before the option that contains the most complete or accurate answer. Check your answers in the Answer Key on page 106.

1. Roy was John's
   ☐ a. classmate.
   ☐ b. friend.
   ☐ c. cousin.
   ☐ d. brother.

2. In the neighborhood, Roy was known as a
   ☐ a. pusher.
   ☐ b. leader.
   ☐ c. troublemaker.
   ☐ d. hustler.

3. When was Roy stabbed?
   - □ a. before the story opened
   - □ b. as soon as the story opened
   - □ c. in the middle of the story
   - □ d. at the end of the story

4. The main point of the story is to show
   - □ a. how John and his family earned a living.
   - □ b. that John was bitter about his family life.
   - □ c. where most black people are forced to live.
   - □ d. the many different feelings of people living in poverty.

5. The relationship between John and his father can be described as
   - □ a. normal.
   - □ b. casual.
   - □ c. troubled.
   - □ d. bold.

6. John reveals his personal plans for the future when he
   - □ a. expresses his dislike for Sarah.
   - □ b. dreads facing his father.
   - □ c. sympathizes with his mother.
   - □ d. whispers in Ruth's ear.

7. Roy was probably injured in
   - □ a. an encounter with the police.
   - □ b. a family argument.
   - □ c. a gang fight.
   - □ d. a grocery store robbery.

8. The atmosphere in John's house was
   - □ a. warm.
   - □ b. religious.
   - □ c. uneasy.
   - □ d. restless.

9. John's father sees himself mainly as
   - □ a. a responsible citizen.
   - □ b. a misunderstood husband.
   - □ c. a good provider.
   - □ d. a man of the Lord.

10. The statement that John's "heart lifted a little" means that he felt
    - □ a. arrogance.
    - □ b. pride.
    - □ c. despair.
    - □ d. hope.

Comprehension Skills

1. recalling specific facts
2. retaining concepts
3. organizing facts
4. understanding the main idea
5. drawing a conclusion
6. making a judgment
7. making an inference
8. recognizing tone
9. understanding characters
10. appreciation of literary forms

Study Skills, Part One—Following is a passage with blanks where words have been omitted. Next to the passage are groups of five words, one group for each blank. Complete the passage by circling the correct word for each of the blanks.

Paragraphs of Illustration

As the name suggests, paragraphs of illustration present examples, illustrations, stories, anecdotes, and so on. They are used by the author to illustrate, clarify, demonstrate, or amplify some idea or concept for the reader. Authors use many paragraphs of illustration to help the reader ___(1)___ the subject.

These paragraphs are also easy to recognize and identify because of the use of key words and phrases like "For example," "An illustration of this," "By way of illustration," and so on. These and ___(2)___ phrases tell the reader that an example or illustrative story is coming up.

Surprisingly, half a chapter, lesson, or article may be ___(3)___ of paragraphs of illustration. Unlike lecturers who are face-to-face with their students, the author is confined by the ___(4)___ of print. The author cannot see the students. He cannot tell how effectively his ideas are coming across. Because the author has no way of knowing this, more illustrations must be used than would be when speaking. He cannot take a chance; it must be ensured that everyone will get the point.

(1) consider   reject
     approve   change   understand

(2) simpler   similar
     familiar   singular   unusual

(3) devoid   disposed
     combined   composed   compared

(4) limitations   inspirations
     exaggeration   situations   aggravation

The writer, too, cannot be questioned over a misunderstood concept; there is no way to pause and __(5)__. It must be certain the first time that the student gets it—there are no second chances. For all of these reasons, we can see why much of what we read is illustrative, even in textbooks.

Selective readers are __(6)__ in their approach. This means that while they may pause over paragraphs of definition, they often speed past paragraphs of illustration. After all, if you understand the point being illustrated, it is not necessary to __(7)__ over additional paragraphs illustrating this same point. You can move on to the place where something new is being presented.

(5)		deny		consider
	clarify		reflect	correct

(6)		lazy		cautious
	confused		flexible	careless

(7)		linger		skip
	pursue		ponder	worry

Study Skills, Part Two—Read the study skills passage again, paying special attention to the lesson being taught. Then, without looking back at the passage, complete each sentence below by writing in the missing word or words. Check the Answer Key on page 106 for the answers to Study Skills, Part One, and Study Skills, Part Two.

1. Paragraphs of illustration are used by the author to help the reader understand an _____ .

2. Because the author cannot see the _____ , he is unable to tell how effectively his ideas are coming across.

3. The writer must be certain that his concepts are not questioned or _____ .

4. Selective readers often _____ past paragraphs of illustration.

5. If you understand the point being illustrated, you can move on to the place where something _____ is being presented.

3 'Tain't So

by Langston Hughes

Vocabulary—The five words below are from the story you are about to read. Study the words and their meanings. Then complete the ten sentences that follow, using one of the five words to fill in the blank in each sentence. Mark your answer by writing the letter of the word on the line before the sentence. Check your answers in the Answer Key on page 106.

A. spry: energetic and physically active

B. customary: common or usual

C. gait: way of walking

D. mellowed: became pleasant and agreeable

E. airs: an attitude of unjustified self-importance

_____ 1. The old lady hobbled along with her cane, her _____ unsteady and halting.

_____ 2. Miss Lucy detested blacks, which caused her to put on _____ in their presence.

_____ 3. Despite her age, Miss Lucy was a _____ lady.

_____ 4. The sunshine felt sweet and warm to Miss Lucy as her violent anger _____ .

_____ 5. It was _____ for the old lady to complain about her many aches and pains.

_____ 6. Spurred on by her boiling anger, Miss Lucy stalked off, her _____ steady and determined.

_____ 7. Miss Cannon kept her old southern views—her attitude toward blacks never _____ .

_____ 8. The old northern white lady did not put on _____ as Miss Lucy did.

_____ 9. For three years the use of a cane had been _____ for Miss Cannon.

_____ 10. Walking like the wind, Miss Lucy felt like the _____ young girl she had once been.

Miss Lucy Cannon was a right nice old white woman, so Uncle Joe always stated, except that she really did *not* like colored folks, not even after she come out West to California. She could never get over certain little southern ways she had, and long as she knowed my Uncle Joe, who hauled her ashes for her, she never would call him *Mister*—nor any other colored man *Mister* neither, for that matter not even the minister of the Baptist Church who was a graduate of San Jose State College. Miss Lucy Cannon just wouldn't call colored folks *Mister* nor Missus, no matter who they was, neither *in* Alabama nor in California.

She was always ailing around, too, sick with first one thing and then another. Delicate, and ever so often she would have a fainting spell, like all good southern white ladies. Looks like the older she got, the more she would be sick and couldn't hardly get around—that is, until she went to a healer and got cured.

And that is one of the funniest stories Uncle Joe ever told me, how old Miss Cannon got cured of her heart and hip in just one cure at the healer's.

Seems like for three years or more she could scarcely walk—even with a cane—had a terrible bad pain in her right leg from her knee up. And on her left side her heart was always just about to give out. She was in bad shape, that old southern lady, to be as spry as she was, always giving teas and dinners and working her colored help to death.

Well, Uncle Joe says, one New Year's Day in Pasadena a friend of hers, a northern lady who was kinda old and retired also and had come out to California to spend her last days, too, and get rid of some parts of her big bank full of money—this old lady told Miss Cannon, "Darling, you just seem to suffer so all the time, and you say you've tried all the doctors and all kinds of baths and medicines. Why don't you try my way of overcoming? Why don't you try faith?"

"Faith, honey?" says old Miss Lucy Cannon, sipping her jasmine tea.

"Yes, my dear," says the northern white lady. "Faith! I have one of the best faith healers in the world."

"Who is he?" asked Miss Lucy Cannon.

"She's a woman, dear," said old Miss Northern White Lady. "And she heals by power. She lives in Hollywood."

"Give me her address," said Miss Lucy, "and I'll go to see her. How much do her treatments cost?"

Miss Lucy warn't so rich as some folks thought she was.

"Only ten dollars, dearest," said the other lady. "Ten dollars a treatment. Go, and you'll come away cured."

"I have never believed in such things," said Miss Lucy, "nor disbelieved, either. But I will go and see." And before she could learn any more about the healer, some other friends came in and interrupted the conversation.

Poor Miss Lucy—her hip was forever giving her grief, her heart forever threatening to give out. But when she sought treatment, the medicine was worse than the malady.

A few days later, however, Miss Lucy took herself all the way from Pasadena to Hollywood, put up for the weekend with a friend of hers, and thought she would go to see the healer, which she did, come Monday morning early.

Using her customary cane and hobbling on her left leg, feeling a bit bad around the heart, and suffering terribly in her mind, she managed to walk slowly but with dignity a half-dozen blocks through the sunshine to the rather humble street in which was located the office and home of the healer.

In spite of the bright morning air and the good breakfast she had had, Miss Lucy (according to herself) felt pretty bad, racked with pains and crippled to the use of a cane.

When she got to the house she was seeking, a large frame dwelling, newly painted, she saw a sign thereon:

MISS PAULINE JONES

"So that's her name," thought Miss Lucy, "Pauline Jones, Miss Jones."

Ring and Enter said a little card above the bell. So Miss Lucy entered. But the first thing that set her back a bit was that nobody received her, so she just sat down to await Miss Jones, the healer who had, she heard, an enormous following in Hollywood. In fact, that's why she had come early, so she wouldn't have to wait long. Now, it was only nine o'clock. The office was open—but empty. So Miss Lucy simply waited. Ten minutes passed. Fifteen. Twenty. Finally she became all nervous and fluttery. Heart and limb! Pain, pain, pain! Not even a magazine to read.

"Oh, me!" she said impatiently. "What is this? Why, I never!"

There was a sign on the wall that read:

BELIEVE

"I will wait just ten minutes more," said Miss Lucy, glancing at her watch of platinum and pearls.

But before the ten minutes were up another woman entered the front door and sat down. To Miss Lucy's horror she was a colored woman! In fact, a big black colored woman!

Said Miss Lucy to herself, "I'll never in the world get used to the North. Now here's a great—my friend says great—faith healer treating darkies! Why, down in Alabama a Negro patient wouldn't dare come in here and sit down with white people like this!"

But, womanlike (and having still five minutes to wait), Miss Lucy couldn't keep her mouth shut that long. She just had to talk, albeit to a Negro, so she began on her favorite subject—herself.

"I certainly feel bad this morning," she said to the colored woman, condescending to open the conversation.

" 'Tain't so," answered the Negro woman placidly, which sort of took Miss Lucy back a bit. She lifted her chin.

"Indeed, it is so," said she indignantly. "My heart is just about to give out. My breath is short."

" 'Tain't so a-tall," commented the colored woman.

"Why!" gasped Miss Lucy. "Such impudence! I tell you *it is so!* I could hardly get down here this morning."

" 'Tain't so," said the woman calmly.

"Besides my heart," went on Miss Lucy, "my right hip pains me so I can hardly sit here."

"I say, 'tain't so."

"I tell you it *is* so," screamed Miss Lucy. "Where is the healer? I won't sit here and suffer this—this impudence. I can't! It'll kill me! It's outrageous."

" 'Tain't so," said the large black woman serenely, whereupon Miss Lucy rose. Her pale face flushed a violent red.

"Where is the healer?" she cried, looking around the room.

"Right here," said the colored woman.

"What?" cried Miss Lucy. "You're the—why—you?"

"I'm Miss Jones."

"Why, I never heard the like," gasped Miss Lucy. "A *colored* woman as famous as you? Why, you must be lying!"

" 'Tain't so," said the woman calmly.

"Well, I shan't stay another minute," cried Miss Lucy.

"Ten dollars, then," said the colored woman. "You've had your treatment, anyhow."

"Ten dollars! That's entirely too much!"

" 'Tain't so."

Angrily Miss Lucy opened her pocketbook, threw a ten-dollar bill on the table, took a deep breath, and bounced out. She went three blocks up Sunset Boulevard, walking like the wind, conversing with herself.

" ' 'Tain't so,' " she muttered. " ' 'Tain't so!' I tell her I'm sick and she says, ' 'Tain't so!' "

Langston Hughes was born in Joplin, Missouri, in 1902. He grew up in Kansas and Colorado, attended Columbia College in New York, and received a degree from Lincoln University in Pennsylvania. Hughes was first recognized as an important literary figure in the 1920s, although much of his early work was criticized by black intellectuals for portraying what they thought to be an unattractive view of black life. For most of his career, Hughes eschewed anger and violence in his writing, relying instead on the use of humor to convey his message. Hughes's works, which include novels, short stories, poems, plays, and two autobiographies, have been translated into many languages. In 1967, Hughes died of congestive heart failure in New York City.

On she went at a rapid gait, stepping like a young girl—so mad she had forgotten all about her infirmities, even her heart—when suddenly she cried, "Lord, have mercy, my cane! For the first time in three years I'm *without* a cane!"

Then she realized that her breath was giving her no trouble at all. Neither was her leg. Her temper mellowed. The sunshine was sweet and warm. She felt good.

"Colored folks do have some funny kind of supernatural conjuring powers, I reckon," she said, smiling to herself. Immediately her face went grim again. "But the impudence of 'em! Soon's they get up North—calling herself *Miss* Pauline Jones. The idea! Putting on airs and charging me ten dollars for a handful of *'tain't so's!*"

In her mind she clearly heard, " 'Tain't so!"

Starting Time		*Finishing Time*		
Reading Time		*Reading Rate*		
Comprehension		*Vocabulary*		

Comprehension— Read the following questions and statements. For each one, put an *x* in the box before the option that contains the most complete or accurate answer. Check your answers in the Answer Key on page 106.

1. Miss Lucy Cannon went to see a
   - ☐ a. medical doctor.
   - ☐ b. college professor.
   - ☐ c. faith healer.
   - ☐ d. protestant minister.

2. Miss Lucy never overcame her
   - ☐ a. femininity.
   - ☐ b. generosity.
   - ☐ c. religion.
   - ☐ d. prejudice.

3. This passage is told as
   - ☐ a. a narrative.
   - ☐ b. an argument.
   - ☐ c. an autobiography.
   - ☐ d. a parable.

4. Miss Jones could cure Lucy Cannon's hip and heart ailments, but she could not cure Miss Cannon's
   - ☐ a. cancer.
   - ☐ b. old age.
   - ☐ c. feelings of racial superiority.
   - ☐ d. habit of giving teas and dinners.

5. Miss Lucy was a little upset when
   - ☐ a. Uncle Joe hauled ashes.
   - ☐ b. she was told to see Miss Jones.
   - ☐ c. no one received her at Miss Jones's.
   - ☐ d. her friend came to visit her.

6. The author implies that the North is to the South as
   - ☐ a. refusal is to hospitality.
   - ☐ b. acceptance is to rejection.
   - ☐ c. outrage is to civility.
   - ☐ d. tolerance is to violence.

7. During the waiting period Miss Lucy was forced to endure, she was probably being
   - ☐ a. abused.
   - ☐ b. observed.
   - ☐ c. humiliated.
   - ☐ d. ridiculed.

8. Uncle Joe's account of Miss Lucy Cannon's adventure is meant to be
   - ☐ a. serious.
   - ☐ b. insulting.
   - ☐ c. racist.
   - ☐ d. humorous.

9. Miss Lucy was
   - ☐ a. an aetheist.
   - ☐ b. a hypochondriac.
   - ☐ c. a hypocrite.
   - ☐ d. an organizer.

10. Langston Hughes's treatment of Miss Lucy Cannon is
   - ☐ a. good-natured.
   - ☐ b. abusive.
   - ☐ c. respectful.
   - ☐ d. filled with bitterness.

Comprehension Skills

1. recalling specific facts	6. making a judgment
2. retaining concepts	7. making an inference
3. organizing facts	8. recognizing tone
4. understanding the main idea	9. understanding characters
5. drawing a conclusion	10. appreciation of literary forms

Study Skills, Part One—Following is a passage with blanks where words have been omitted. Next to the passage are groups of five words, one group for each blank. Complete the passage by circling the correct word for each of the blanks.

Paragraphs of Information

The next paragraphs we wish to examine are the ones used by the author to pass along information on the __(1)__ . For this reason they are called paragraphs of information. These paragraphs contain names, dates, details, facts, explanations, and other factual information.

In a particular chapter or lesson, the reader can expect to find the meat of the matter in paragraphs like these. This is where the author gets down to business and presents the __(2)__ . The essential terms have been defined and illustrated and now the reader is ready for the substance of the lesson.

We ask the reader to recognize paragraphs of information because they contain the instructional material he is responsible for. Here is where the data is found that he will be __(3)__ on later.

In presenting information the author will probably use one of the following methods of development.

1. State an opinion and give reasons. Look for a clue word used to __(4)__ a series of reasons.

2. Pose a problem and offer a solution. Authors use this method frequently because it incorporates questioning as an aid to learning.

3. Draw a conclusion and then present proof. Actually the proof may come first, preceding the conclusion. Check to be sure that the conclusion __(5)__ follows from the proof.

(1) edition   subject
     reader   students   teacher

(2) aims   conclusions
     facts   introductions   outline

(3) examined   contained
     judged   instructed   prepared

(4) overcome   introduce
     produce   prove   deny

(5) loosely   systematically
     ideally   logically   hopefully

4. Present steps in an argument. ___(6)___ here, too, an enumeration. Look for the introductory signal and circle the enumerations.

5. Make a comparison or draw a contrast. Frequently used in paragraphs of illustration, this method may be used to ___(7)___ information, too.

The paragraphs of information are the heart of the lesson. Study them well.

(6)   Delete   Reject
     Create   Expect   Ignore

(7)   repeat   withhold
        deny   restrict   present

Study Skills, Part Two—Read the study skills passage again, paying special attention to the lesson being taught. Then, without looking back at the passage, complete each sentence below by writing in the missing word or words. Check the Answer Key on page 106 for the answers to Study Skills, Part One, and Study Skills, Part Two.

1. In paragraphs of information, the author gets down to business and presents the _____ of the matter.

2. The reader will find data and _____ material in these paragraphs.

3. In a paragraph of information, the author may state an opinion and give _____ .

4. An author may pose a problem and offer a solution, because this method uses questioning as an aid to _____ .

5. Paragraphs of information are very important. One should _____ them well.

4 Jubilee

by Margaret Walker

Vocabulary—The five words below are from the story you are about to read. Study the words and their meanings. Then complete the ten sentences that follow, using one of the five words to fill in the blank in each sentence. Mark your answer by writing the letter of the word on the line before the sentence. Check your answers in the Answer Key on page 106.

A. crib: a storage bin for corn

B. scrupulously: carefully, conscientiously

C. fault: to an extreme; as in *generous to a fault*

D. congenial: having the same feelings; existing together in harmony

E. haunting: on one's mind constantly; recurring spontaneously

_____ 1. At Christmas everyone displayed a _____ mood.

_____ 2. A _____ feeling that this kindness was short-lived came to every slave's mind.

_____ 3. Big Missy seemed more _____ than ever at Christmas.

_____ 4. It was the time of year when Marster was kind to a _____ .

_____ 5. By the time winter arrived, the harvest had been completed and the corn was safely stored in Marster's _____ .

_____ 6. For years, the routine of _____ gathering the harvest had been carried out by the slaves.

_____ 7. Throughout the winter, grain from the _____ would supply the plantation with freshly ground meal.

_____ 8. Stolen food and goodies were _____ hidden within the slave cabins.

_____ 9. Everyone from the plantation owner to the lowliest slave was generous to a _____ at Christmastime.

_____ 10. The _____ tunes sung by the slaves caused Marse John and his family to weep.

"There's a star in the East on Christmas morn"

Christmas time on the plantation was always the happiest time of the year. Harvest time was over. The molasses had been made. Marster's corn was in his crib and the slaves' new corn meal had been ground. Lye, hominy and sauerkraut were packed away in big jars and stone or clay crocks. Elderberry, blackberry, poke weed and dandelion, black cherry and scuppernong, muscatine and wild plum, crab apple and persimmon, all had been picked and made into jars of jelly, jam, preserves, and kegs of wine. There were persimmon beer and home-made corn likker, and a fermented home brew for future use. Despite Big Missy's clever vigilance with her ipecac, some of those jars of jelly and preserves and peach brandy had inevitably gone out of the pantry window into the waiting fingers of black hands. What the slaves could not conveniently steal, they begged and made for themselves. Many of the delicacies that they loved were free for the taking in the woods. Who did not know how to mix the dark brown sugar or black cane molasses or sorghum with various fruits and berries to make the good wine and brew the beer and whiskey from the corn or rye that every clever finger learned early how to snatch and hide? When the frost turned the leaves and the wind blew them from the trees, it was time to go into the woods and gather nuts, hickory nuts and black walnuts, and chinkapinks. There were always more pecans on the place than could be eaten and the hogs rooted out the rotting ones. If Marster had not given them a goober patch, they had patches of goober peas around their cabins anyway. Sometimes there were whole fields of these wonderful peanuts. Like the industrious squirrels around them they scrupulously gathered the wild harvest and wrapped them in rags, laying-by their knick-knacks for the long winter nights. When the autumn haze ended and the chilling winter winds descended upon them it was time to hunt the possum and to catch a coon. No feast during the Christmas holidays would be good without a possum and a coon. Of course, Vyry said, "You got to know how to cook it, or it ain't no good. You got to boil that wild taste out with red-hot pepper and strong vinegar made out of sour apple peelings and plenty salt. You got to boil it in one water and then take it out and boil it in another water, and you got to soak the blood out first overnight and clean it real good so you gits all the blood out and you got to scrape all the hair left from the least bit of hide and then you got to roast it a long, slow time until you poured all that fat grease off and roast sweet potatoes soft and sugary, and if that stuff don't make you hit your mama till she holler and make you slobber all over yourself, they's something wrong with you and the almighty God didn't make you at the right time of the year. Marster, he like foxes, but what good is a fox when

A slave's Christmas promised everything that was missing the year round: food, drink, music, fun, and rest.

you can't eat him? Make sense to catch varmints stealing chickens, foxes and wolves, for that matter, and it's good to catch an old black bear, or a ferocity vicious bobcat, and nasty old varmint like a weasel when he come sneaking around, but when you hunting for meat and you wants fresh meat, kill the rabbit and the coon, kill the squirrel and the possum and I'll sho-nuff be satisfied."

If the slave did not kill his meat, he wasn't likely to eat fresh meat, although at hog-killing time they were given the tubs of chitterlings, the liver and the lights, and sometimes even the feet. After a very good harvest Marster might let them have a young shoat to barbecue, especially at Christmas time. Marse John was generous to a fault and always gave plenty of cheap rum and gallons of cheap whiskey to wash the special Christmas goodies down.

Big Missy had a taste for wild game too, but it was quail and pheasant, wild turkey and wild ducks, and occasionally the big fat bucks that came out of their own woods for wonderful roasts of venison. The Negros were not allowed to kill these and if they made a mistake and accidentally killed birds or deer they had better not be caught eating it. Vyry had learned from Aunt Sally how to lard quail with salt fat pork and how to cook potted pheasant in cream, to roast and stuff turkey and geese and ducks, but she knew also the penalty for even tasting such morsels if Big Missy found out about it. Sometimes, however, half a turkey or goose was stolen from the springhouse, after some expert had carefully picked the lock. Most of the time, however, they did not worry about Big Missy's game as long as they could get enough of what they could put into their hands while foraging through the woods. By some uncanny and unknown reason real white flour came from somewhere for Christmas, and eggs were hoarded from a stray nest for egg bread instead of plain corn pone, but real butter cake and meat and fruit pies were seldom found in a slave cabin. Sometimes on Christmas they tasted snacks of real goodies such as these as part of their Christmas. On Christmas morning all the field hands stood outside the Big House shouting, "Christmas gift, Christmas gift, Marster." Then, and only then, did they taste fresh citrus fruit. Every slave child on the place received an orange, hard Christmas candy, and sometimes ginger cake. There were snuff and chewing tobacco for the women, whiskey and rum for the men. Sometimes there were new clothes, but generally the shoes were given out in November before Thanksgiving.

On Christmas morning there was always a warm and congenial relationship between the Big House and the slave Quarters. If it was cold, and very often it was not, the slaves huddled in rags and shawls around their heads and shoulders, and Marse John would open his front door and come out on the veranda. His guests and family and poor white kin, who were always welcomed in the house at Christmas time, came out with him and gathered round to hear his annual Christmas speech to the slaves. He thanked them for such a good crop and working so hard and faithfully, said it was good to have them all together, and good to enjoy Christmas together when they all had been so good. He talked about the meaning of Christmas—"When I was a boy on this very place at Christmas time, seems only yesterday . . ." He got sentimental about his father and mother, and he told a "darkey" joke or two, and then he wished them a merry Christmas, ordered whiskey and rum for everyone, handed out their gifts of candy and oranges and snuff and tobacco, and asked them to sing a song, please, for him and his family and all their guests. Then they sang their own moving Christmas carols, "Wasn't that a mighty day when Jesus Christ was born" and "Go tell it on the Mountain that Jesus Christ is born" and the especially haunting melody that everybody loved:

> There's a star in the East
> on Christmas morn,
> Rise up shepherds and foller,
> It'll lead to the place where
> the Savior's born,
> Rise up shepherds and foller.

Then Marse John and all his white family and their friends would wipe their weeping eyes and blow their running noses and go inside to the good Christmas breakfast of fried chicken and waffles and steaming black coffee with

Margaret Walker studied at Northwestern University, majoring in English, and received her M.A. in 1940 from the University of Iowa. In 1942, Walker's book *For My People* was published as selection of the year in the Yale University Series of Younger Poets. She was awarded a fellowship at the University of Iowa in 1963, where she received a Ph.D. and completed her novel *Jubilee*.

Walker taught English at Livingstone College and West Virginia State College and has been a member of the faculty at Jackson State University in Mississippi since 1949.

fresh clotted cream. And the slaves, happy with the rest that came with the season, went back to their cabins, certain that for one day of the year at least they would have enough to eat. They could hardly wait for night and the banjo parties to begin. On Marse John's plantation, Christmas was always an occasion and all during the holidays there were dancing parties and dinners with lots of wonderful food and plenty of the finest liquor. Marse John and Big Missy became celebrated for their fine turkeys and English fruit cakes and puddings, duffs full of sherry and brandy, excellent sillabub and eggnog, all prepared by their well-trained servants, who cooked and served their Master's fare with a flourish.

Starting Time		Finishing Time	
Reading Time		Reading Rate	
Comprehension		Vocabulary	

Comprehension— Read the following questions and statements. For each one, put an *x* in the box before the option that contains the most complete or accurate answer. Check your answers in the Answer Key on page 106.

1. Vyry learned how to cook wild game from
   - ☐ a. Marse John.
   - ☐ b. Big Missy.
   - ☐ c. Little Louis.
   - ☐ d. Aunt Sally.

2. The slaves managed to get special food and drink
   - ☐ a. through stealth.
   - ☐ b. from the larder.
   - ☐ c. from Big Missy.
   - ☐ d. from neighbors.

3. The way of life described in this story fits into which of the following periods?
   - ☐ a. around the early 1600s
   - ☐ b. before the American Civil War
   - ☐ c. the late 1800s
   - ☐ d. just before Prohibition

4. Christmas on the plantation was a time of
   - ☐ a. celebration by all.
   - ☐ b. resentment.
   - ☐ c. equal sharing among owners and slaves.
   - ☐ d. indifference.

5. The life of the plantation owner was
   - □ a. sentimental and religious.
   - □ b. comfortable and secure.
   - □ c. violent and warlike.
   - □ d. virtuous and rewarding.

6. Considering how the slaves were treated the rest of the year, the traditional Christmas morning gathering on Marse John's veranda can be seen as being
   - □ a. hollow and hypocritical.
   - □ b. sensitive and caring.
   - □ c. a typical day.
   - □ d. the dawn of a new approach toward the slaves.

7. This selection suggests that
   - □ a. slaves could not cook well.
   - □ b. Christmas was a time for quiet prayer.
   - □ c. no one on the plantation could sing.
   - □ d. Marster John was not always so generous.

8. The overall tone of this selection is one of
   - □ a. fond remembrance.
   - □ b. aggravation.
   - □ c. antagonism.
   - □ d. humor at the narrator's own expense.

9. Marse John is represented as being
   - □ a. indifferent.
   - □ b. not so much cruel as distant.
   - □ c. mean and stingy every day of the year but one.
   - □ d. reliable.

10. The expression "Like the industrious squirrels around them . . ." makes use of
   - □ a. an idiom.
   - □ b. a contrast.
   - □ c. a metaphor.
   - □ d. a simile.

Comprehension Skills

1. recalling specific facts	6. making a judgment
2. retaining concepts	7. making an inference
3. organizing facts	8. recognizing tone
4. understanding the main idea	9. understanding characters
5. drawing a conclusion	10. appreciation of literary forms

Study Skills, Part One—Following is a passage with blanks where words have been omitted. Next to the passage are groups of five words, one group for each blank. Complete the passage by circling the correct word for each of the blanks.

Paragraphs of Definition

We have seen how authors use their paragraphs of introduction to "kick off" the article or chapter and to introduce the reader to the subject or ___(1)___ .

The next paragraph we are going to examine is the one used to define or explain an idea or concept that is ___(2)___ to the reader.

Fortunately paragraphs of definition are easily recognizable. Frequently, the word, phrase, or concept being defined is shown in italics—this tells the reader that the word or words in italics are being studied and analyzed. Certain key words appear regularly in these paragraphs, words authors use when defining. Look for phrases like "We can define this as . . ." or "This simply means . . ." and similar phrases, often including the word "define."

It is ___(3)___ that the reader recognize these paragraphs because what is defined is important to know and understand. The reader can be certain that much of what is to follow may hinge on his or her understanding of the new word or concept.

Students should study carefully each word of the definition because every word is loaded with essential

(1)   title   introduction
     preface   topic   illustration

(2)   difficult   familiar
     new   unnecessary   old

(3)   essential   evident
     obvious   unusual   useful

information. The reason for this is that definitions are by nature __(4)__ constructed. The words have been carefully selected to convey the exact meaning that the concept demands. The greatest mistake a student can make is to hurry past a __(5)__ . Look at the contribution of each word to the total meaning.

Question the author: "What exactly does this word add to the meaning? How would the definition change with this word left out?" The wise student always pauses and rereads definitions, at least once. No other single paragraph may be so essential to __(6)__ of the chapter.

Paragraphs of definition appear often in textbooks. __(7)__ , they are of extreme value to the student.

(4)   loosely   independently
   professionally   partially   precisely

(5)   chapter   character
   sentence   definition   statement

(6)   comparison   continuation
   comprehension   completion   extension

(7)   Conveniently   Rarely
   Substantially   Consequently   Eventually

Study Skills, Part Two—Read the study skills passage again, paying special attention to the lesson being taught. Then, without looking back at the passage, complete each sentence below by writing in the missing word or words. Check the Answer Key on page 106 for the answers to Study Skills, Part One, and Study Skills, Part Two.

1. Paragraphs of definition are easily _____ .

2. Words being studied or analyzed are frequently shown in

   _____ .

3. Authors use certain _____ words when they are defining things.

4. Students should carefully study each word of the definition, because every

   word is a source of essential _____ .

5. To capture the total meaning of a definition, look at the _____

   of each word.

5 # Up From Slavery

by Booker T. Washington

Vocabulary—The five words below are from the story you are about to read. Study the words and their meanings. Then complete the ten sentences that follow, using one of the five words to fill in the blank in each sentence. Mark your answer by writing the letter of the word on the line before the sentence. Check your answers in the Answer Key on page 106.

A. pretentious: sophisticated; ambitious

B. grave: serious, of some importance

C. consumed: used up

D. indispensable: absolutely necessary

E. prevailing: happening most often, dominant

_____ 1. Being poor has created many _____ situations for the black man, both past and present.

_____ 2. Washington knew that an education was _____ if he was to better himself.

_____ 3. When the teachers realized how _____ the young Washington's situation was, they brought him secondhand clothes.

_____ 4. The school at Hampton was much more _____ than the school back home was.

_____ 5. Washington _____ the textbooks at a tremendous pace and still hungered for more.

_____ 6. As janitor of Hampton School, Washington was determined to prove his worth and make his services _____ .

_____ 7. The desire to learn was Washington's _____ feeling.

_____ 8. As soon as Washington's last penny had been _____ , he was hired out as a dockworker.

_____ 9. Most of the students picked up on the _____ air of the instructor.

_____ 10. To better the conditions of the people they had left at home was the _____ idea among the students.

One day, while at work in the coal-mine, I happened to overhear two miners talking about a great school for coloured people somewhere in Virginia. This was the first time that I had ever heard anything about any kind of school or college that was more pretentious than the little coloured school in our town.

In the darkness of the mine I noiselessly crept as close as I could to the two men who were talking. I heard one tell the other that not only was the school established for the members of my race, but that opportunities were provided by which poor but worthy students could work out all or a part of the cost of board, and at the same time be taught some trade or industry.

As they went on describing the school, it seemed to me that it must be the greatest place on earth, and not even Heaven presented more attractions for me at that time than did the Hampton Normal and Agricultural Institute in Virginia, about which those men were talking. I resolved at once to go to that school, although I had no idea where it was, or how many miles away, or how I was going to reach it; I remembered only that I was on fire constantly with one ambition, and that was to go to Hampton. This thought was with me day and night. . . .

In the fall of 1872 I determined to make an effort to get there, although, as I have stated, I had no definite idea of the direction in which Hampton was, or of what it would cost to go there. I do not think that any one thoroughly sympathized with me in my ambition to go to Hampton unless it was my mother, and she was troubled with a grave fear that I was starting out on a "wild-goose chase." At any rate, I got only a half-hearted consent from her that I might start. The small amount of money that I had earned had been consumed by my stepfather and the remainder of the family, with the exception of a very few dollars, and so I had very little with which to buy clothes and pay my travelling expenses. My brother John helped me all that he could, but of course that was not a great deal, for his work was in the coal-mine, where he did not earn much, and most of what he did earn went in the direction of paying the household expenses.

Perhaps the thing that touched and pleased me most in connection with my starting for Hampton was the interest that many of the older coloured people took in the matter. They had spent the best days of their lives in slavery, and hardly expected to live to see the time when they would see a member of their race leave home to attend a boarding-school. Some of these older people would give me a nickel, others a quarter, or a handkerchief.

Finally the great day came, and I started for Hampton. I had only a small, cheap satchel that contained what few articles of clothing I could get. My mother at the time was rather weak and broken in health. I hardly expected

Young Booker T. Washington resolved to go to the Hampton Institute even before he knew where it was. When he found out the school was 500 miles away, he set off anyway . . . on foot.

to see her again, and thus our parting was all the more sad. She, however, was very brave through it all. At that time there were no through trains connecting that part of West Virginia with eastern Virginia. Trains ran only a portion of the way, and the remainder of the distance was travelled by stage-coaches.

The distance from Malden to Hampton is about five hundred miles. I had not been away from home many hours before it began to grow painfully evident that I did not have enough money to pay my fare to Hampton. . . .

By walking, begging rides both in wagons and in the cars, in some way, after a number of days, I reached the city of Richmond, Virginia, about eighty-two miles from Hampton. When I reached there, tired, hungry, and dirty, it was late in the night. I had never been in a large city, and this rather added to my misery. . . . I was completely out of money. . . .

I must have walked the streets till after midnight. At last I became so exhausted that I could walk no longer. I was tired. I was hungry, I was everything but discouraged. Just about the time when I reached extreme physical exhaustion, I came upon a portion of a street where the board sidewalk was considerably elevated. I waited for a few minutes, till I was sure that no passers-by could see me, and then crept under the sidewalk and lay for the night upon the ground, with my satchel of clothing for a pillow. Nearly all night I could hear the tramp of feet over my head. The next morning I found myself somewhat refreshed, but was extremely hungry, because it had been a long time since I had had sufficient food. As soon as it became light enough for me to see my surroundings, I noticed that I was near a large ship, and that this ship seemed to be unloading a cargo of pig iron. I went at once to the vessel and asked the captain to permit me to help unload the vessel in order to get money for food. The captain, a white man, who seemed to be kind-hearted, consented. I worked long enough to earn money for my breakfast, and it seems to me, as I remember it now, to have been about the best breakfast that I have ever eaten.

My work pleased the captain so well that he told me if I desired I could continue working for a small amount per day. This I was very glad to do. I continued working on this vessel for a number of days. After buying food with the small wages I received there was not much left to add to the amount I must get to pay my way to Hampton. In order to economize in every way possible, so as to be sure to reach Hampton in a reasonable time, I continued to sleep under the same sidewalk that gave me shelter the first night I was in Richmond. . . .

When I had saved what I considered enough money with which to reach Hampton, I thanked the captain of the vessel for his kindness, and started again. Without any unusual occurrence I reached Hampton, with a surplus of exactly fifty cents with which to begin my education. To me it had been a long, eventful journey; but the first sight of the large, three-story, brick school building seemed to have rewarded me for all that I had undergone in order to reach the place. . . . It seemed to me to be the largest and most beautiful building I had ever seen. The sight of it seemed to give me new life. I felt that a new kind of existence had now begun—that life would now have a new meaning. I felt that I had reached the promised land, and I resolved to let no obstacle prevent me from putting forth the highest effort to fit myself to accomplish the most good in the world. . . .

Life at Hampton was a constant revelation to me; was constantly taking me into a new world. The matter of having meals at regular hours, of eating on a tablecloth, using a napkin, the use of the bathtub and of the tooth-brush, as well as the use of sheets upon the bed, were all new to me. . . .

The charge for my board at Hampton was ten dollars per month. I was expected to pay a part of this in cash and to work out the remainder. To meet this cash payment, as I have stated, I had just fifty cents when I reached the institution. Aside from a very few dollars that my brother John was able to send me once in a while, I had no money with which to pay my board. I was determined from the first to make my work as janitor so valuable that my services would be indispensable. This I succeeded in doing to such an extent that I was soon informed that I would be allowed the full cost of my board in return for my work. The cost of tuition was seventy dollars a year. This, of course, was wholly beyond my ability to provide. If I had been compelled to pay the seventy dollars for tuition, in addition to providing for my board, I would have been compelled to leave the Hampton school. General Armstrong, however, very kindly got Mr. S. Griffitts Morgan, of New Bedford, Mass., to defray the cost of my tuition during the whole time that I was at Hampton. . . .

After having been for a while at Hampton, I found myself in difficulty because I did not have books and clothing. Usually, however, I got around the trouble about books by borrowing from those who were more fortunate than myself. As to clothes, when I reached Hampton I had practically nothing. Everything that I possessed was in the small hand satchel. . . .

In some way I managed to get on till the teachers learned that I was in earnest and meant to succeed, and then some of them were kind enough to see that I was partly supplied with second-hand clothing that had been sent in barrels from the North. These barrels proved a blessing to hundreds of poor but deserving students. Without them I question whether I should ever have gotten through Hampton. . . .

I was among the youngest of the students who were in Hampton at that time. Most of the students were men and women—some as old as forty years of age. As I now

Booker T. Washington was the most influential black leader and educator of his time in the United States. Born a slave in 1856, he was freed by the United States government in 1865 and attended the Hampton Institute, an industrial school for blacks in Virginia, from 1872 to 1875. Washington became a teacher at Hampton in 1879, then founded the Tuskegee Institute, a vocational school for blacks in Alabama.

Washington's educational and political philosophies were criticized by some, notably, sociologist and historian W. E. B. DuBois. Washington believed that blacks could benefit more from a practical, vocational education than from the college education espoused by DuBois. He felt black people should work hard, acquire property, and develop a strong economic foundation. In turn, he believed, civil and political rights would be granted to blacks. In keeping with his moderate stance, Washington never publicly supported black political causes. He did, however, secretly finance lawsuits opposing segregation. Washington remained a powerful leader until his death in 1915.

recall the scene of my first year, I do not believe that one often has the opportunity of coming into contact with three or four hundred men and women who were so tremendously in earnest as these men and women were. Every hour was occupied in study or work. Nearly all had had enough actual contact with the world to teach them the need of education. Many of the older ones were, of course, too old to master the textbooks very thoroughly, and it was often sad to watch their struggles; but they made up in earnestness much of what they lacked in books. Many of them were as poor as I was, and, besides having to wrestle with their books, they had to struggle with a poverty which prevented their having the necessities of life. Many of them had aged parents who were dependent upon them, and some of them were men who had wives whose support in some way they had to provide for.

The great and prevailing idea that seemed to take possession of every one was to prepare himself to lift up the people at his home. No one seemed to think of himself. And the officers and teachers, what a rare set of human beings they were! They worked for the students night and day, in season and out of season. They seemed happy only when they were helping students in some manner. Whenever it is written—and I hope it will be—the part that the Yankee teachers played in the education of the Negroes immediately after the war will make one of the most thrilling parts of the history of this country.

Starting Time		Finishing Time	
Reading Time		Reading Rate	
Comprehension		Vocabulary	

Comprehension— Read the following questions and statements. For each one, put an *x* in the box before the option that contains the most complete or accurate answer. Check your answers in the Answer Key on page 106.

1. Booker T. Washington was raised in
   - ☐ a. Malden, West Virginia.
   - ☐ b. Richmond, Virginia.
   - ☐ c. Hampton, Virginia.
   - ☐ d. Roanoke, Virginia.

2. The teachers at Hampton were
   - ☐ a. sensitive to the needs of the students.
   - ☐ b. impressed with black intellectuals.
   - ☐ c. in tune with the ideas of the community.
   - ☐ d. concerned with economic gain.

3. The events in this selection are presented in
   - ☐ a. order of importance.
   - ☐ b. numerical order.
   - ☐ c. spatial order.
   - ☐ d. chronological order.

4. Which of the following best expresses the theme of the selection?
   - ☐ a. Slow and steady wins the race.
   - ☐ b. To reap, one must sow.
   - ☐ c. The truth shall set men free.
   - ☐ d. Virtue is its own reward.

5. Which of the following seems to be true?
   - ☐ a. Hampton was a short distance from Malden.
   - ☐ b. Washington's family was poor.
   - ☐ c. Mr. Morgan was Washington's uncle.
   - ☐ d. General Armstrong disliked Washington.

6. The Yankee teachers at Hampton
   - ☐ a. refused to teach black children.
   - ☐ b. were not prejudiced toward blacks.
   - ☐ c. made better teachers than southern teachers.
   - ☐ d. were better educated than most teachers.

7. There is evidence to suggest that the Hampton Normal and Agricultural Institute received support from
   - ☐ a. the federal government.
   - ☐ b. black organizations.
   - ☐ c. the state of Virginia.
   - ☐ d. Northern whites.

8. The tone of the selection is meant to be
   - ☐ a. depressing.
   - ☐ b. ironic.
   - ☐ c. factual.
   - ☐ d. inspiring.

9. The selection suggests that Washington was
   - ☐ a. remarkable, despite average ability.
   - ☐ b. poor, hungry, and lonely.
   - ☐ c. ingenious, talented, and industrious.
   - ☐ d. insensitive to his family's needs.

10. The selection can best be classified as being
    - ☐ a. narrative.
    - ☐ b. biographical.
    - ☐ c. autobiographical.
    - ☐ d. descriptive.

Comprehension Skills

1. recalling specific facts	6. making a judgment
2. retaining concepts	7. making an inference
3. organizing facts	8. recognizing tone
4. understanding the main idea	9. understanding characters
5. drawing a conclusion	10. appreciation of literary forms

Study Skills, Part One—Following is a passage with blanks where words have been omitted. Next to the passage are groups of five words, one group for each blank. Complete the passage by circling the correct word for each of the blanks.

Paragraphs of Transition

The recognizable feature of paragraphs of transition is their brevity—they are normally short.

As the name ___(1)___ , these paragraphs are used by the author to pass logically from one aspect of the subject to another. Through paragraphs of transition authors show a change of thought or introduce a new side to the matter under discussion.

(1)   reveals   implies
    injects   intends   insists

The reader should be alert to an upcoming ___(2)___ when he sees a paragraph of transition. He should know the author is about to switch tracks and change to a new topic. This knowledge helps the student to organize the reading because it is obvious that the current discussion is ending and that something new is coming.

Transitional paragraphs are valuable in other ways, too. Because they introduce something new, they may function as a paragraph of introduction—they may offer a brief ___(3)___ of the new concepts the author now plans to discuss; they may state the purpose the author hopes to accomplish by presenting the following information; or they may try to ___(4)___ the reader's interest in what is to follow.

In another way, paragraphs of transition may function as a concluding paragraph, ___(5)___ up for the reader the salient points of the aspect being concluded. Or a restatement of the central thought may be presented to help the reader understand the subject before moving on.

It is this combination of functions and its ___(6)___ to the reader's organization that makes this brief paragraph so valuable.

Because in any well-written presentation the paragraphs have certain jobs or functions to perform, a knowledge of paragraph ___(7)___ is valuable to the reader.

(2)	change		translation
	correction	discussion	persuasion

(3)	suggestion		addition
	rejection	condition	preview

(4)	confuse		retain
	arouse	discourage	delay

(5)	pointing		summing
	looking	closing	opening

(6)	statement		continuation
	tribute	contribution	suggestion

(7)	areas		situations
	conditions	conclusions	roles

Study Skills, Part Two—Read the study skills passage again, paying special attention to the lesson being taught. Then, without looking back at the passage, complete each sentence below by writing in the missing word or words. Check the Answer Key on page 106 for the answers to Study Skills, Part One, and Study Skills, Part Two.

1. Paragraphs of transition are normally _____ .

2. The reader knows that the current discussion is _____ when he sees a paragraph of transition.

3. Paragraphs of transition sometimes function as paragraphs of _____ when they state new concepts the author plans to discuss.

4. These paragraphs may be used as _____ paragraphs when they restate a central thought before moving on.

5. The paragraph of transition is valuable to the reader because it has a combination of _____ .

6 | Die, Nigger, Die

by H. Rap Brown

Vocabulary—The five words below are from the story you are about to read. Study the words and their meanings. Then complete the ten sentences that follow, using one of the five words to fill in the blank in each sentence. Mark your answer by writing the letter of the word on the line before the sentence. Check your answers in the Answer Key on page 106.

A. inciting: arousing to action

B. bound: obliged

C. consciousness: awareness of what is in one's own mind

D. pinnacle: the peak, the highest aspiration

E. mount: to initiate an attack or campaign

_____ 1. The white people's _____ of the plight of black people needs to be raised.

_____ 2. Brown was the first to admit that he was jailed for _____ a riot.

_____ 3. The _____ of any person's desire is to be free.

_____ 4. The day will come, according to Brown, when the black man's _____ will be aroused, and spurred into action.

_____ 5. In some cases, our society can _____ an all out assault against minor crimes.

_____ 6. Jailing Brown did not silence his letters _____ people to act.

_____ 7. The white population is _____ to listen, one way or another, to the concerns of black people.

_____ 8. To _____ an investigation against the legal genocide in the courts would be one step toward equality.

_____ 9. The quest of the black man can never be abandoned until the last _____ is attained.

_____ 10. According to Brown, the black man is not _____ to obey the laws made by white men.

While I was in jail in Alexandria, I wrote what was to become a series of Letters from Jail. I didn't plan it like that but that's how it's been working out. I feel when I'm in jail that the people should understand very clearly that the reason I'm in jail is because my crime is political, because I've spoken out against injustices. When I was arrested after Cambridge, the press tried to portray me as some kind of dangerous outlaw. So in my Letters from Jail, I raised the question: Who Are the Real Outlaws?

In this letter from jail, H. Rap Brown rips away the veil obscuring the lies and repression of an "illegal government."

Brothers and Sisters,

White people are saying that the uprisings of our people in almost 100 american cities "must be a conspiracy." Where is the real conspiracy? *Black people across this country have known that the real conspiracy in this country is to run us out, keep us down or kill us, if we can't act like the honky wants us to act.*

We're fighting for our survival and for this we are called criminals, outlaws and murderers. Who are the real criminals? *Who stole us from Africa? Who has been stealing our labor these past 400 years to build this country?* Who are the real murderers? *Why don't they call the police who gun us down in the streets every day, all year 'round . . . why don't they call them murderers?*

Why don't they call Lyndon Johnson a murderer and an outlaw? He fights an illegal war with our brothers and our sons. He sends them to fight against other people of color who are also fighting for their freedom.

Who are the real outlaws in this country? *They say I am an outlaw. I am charged with inciting Black people to "riot." It is against the "law" to riot. But did you or I have any say in passing this law? Do we have much of a say in any of the laws passed in this country? I consider myself neither morally nor legally bound to obey laws that were made by a group of white "lawmakers" who did not let my people be represented in making those laws.*

That government which makes laws that you and I are supposed to obey, without letting us be a part of that government . . . is an illegal government. The men who pass those laws are outlaws; the police who enforce those laws are outlaws and murderers.

It should be understandable that we, as Black people, should adopt the attitude that we are neither morally nor legally bound to obey laws which were not made with our consent and which seek to keep us "in our place." Nor can we be expected to have confidence in the white man's courts which interpret and enforce those laws. The white man makes all the laws, he drags us before his courts, he accuses us, and he sits in judgment over us.

White america should not fool itself into believing that if it comes down harder on us that that will keep us from doing what we believe is right. History has shown that when a man's consciousness is aroused, when a man really believes what he is doing, threats of jail and death cannot turn that man back. The threat of jail or death will not turn me nor others like me from the path we have taken.

We stand on the eve of a Black revolution. These rebellions are but a dress rehearsal for real revolution. For to men, freedom in their own land is the pinnacle of their ambitions, and nothing can turn men aside who have conviction and a strong sense of freedom.

More powerful than my fear of what could happen to me in prison is my hatred for what happens to my people in those outside prisons called the Black ghettoes of this country. I hate the practice of race discrimination, and in my hatred I am supported by the fact that the overwhelming majority of mankind hates it equally. There is nothing any court can do to me that will change that hatred in me; it can only be changed by the removal of the racism and inhumanity which exists in this country.

A society which can mount a huge military action against a Black youth who breaks a window, and at the same time plead that it is powerless to protect Black youths who are being murdered each year because they seek to make democracy in america a reality, is a sick, criminal and insane society. They talk about violence in the country's streets! Each time a Black church is bombed or burned, that is violence in our streets! Where are the troops?

Each time a Black body is found in the swamps of Mississippi or Alabama, that is violence in our land! Where are those murderers?

Each time Black human rights workers are refused protection by the government, that is anarchy!

Each time a police officer shoots and kills a Black teenager, that is urban crime! Where is the national leader who will go on t.v. and condemn police crime?

Black people see america for what it is. It is clear now that white america cannot condemn itself, cannot see the reality of its crimes against mankind. We see america for what it is: the Fourth Reich . . . and we recognize our course of action.

The repeated attempts that the government has made to silence me represent just one level of genocide that is practiced by america. This genocide can be seen on many different levels. It can be seen actively in Vietnam where 45 percent of the frontline casualties are Black. That's no accident. Another level of genocide can be seen operating in the South, where many Black people live on a starvation level. Over 500 Black people die in Alabama each year for lack of proper food and nourishment. This is happening in a country that sends people to the moon. Yet another level of genocide can be seen in the courts. Any Black man across america who faces a white judge or who faces any court procedure can expect the maximum fine and the maximum sentence. Muhammad Ali, LeRoi

Jones, Huey Newton, Ed Oquenda, myself, and thousands of Black men and women across the country have been thrown into prison because we have stood up and challenged the system. Some of the best minds in the Black community are in jail and that's genocide. The most obvious example of genocide is in the concentration camps that america has prepared for Black people. This came about as a result of the McCarran Act of 1950, a law that establishes concentration camps. There is a part, Title II, which suspends the right of due process. That means that there goes the dissolution of all machinery whereby you would be entitled to see a lawyer or go to court. You're arrested and taken off to the camp, without having had an opportunity to state your side of the case. Not that the presentation of your case matters.

At the present time, america still lets us use her "legal" machinery and, through legal maneuvers, my attorney was able to get me freed. But this was only after the court set ridiculously high bail. This is nothing short of ransom. I anticipate one day, however, that I will be arrested and there will be no legal procedure any lawyer will be able to use to secure my release. In fact, the first question will not be, Let's get Rap out of jail. It'll be, Where is Rap?

American political activist and author H. Rap Brown was a controversial civil rights figure during the '60s and early '70s. Born in Baton Rouge, Louisiana, in 1943, Brown was raised in an orphanage by white missionaries. At fifteen he entered Southern University and became active in the civil rights movement. Brown was the most revolutionary of the leaders of the Student Nonviolent Coordinating Committee, and replaced Stokely Carmichael as chairman in 1967. He also served as minister of justice for the Black Panthers organization, often giving speeches advocating black militancy and rebellious confrontations. In 1970, Brown was jailed on charges of arson and inciting a riot in Cambridge, Maryland.

Starting Time	Finishing Time
Reading Time	Reading Rate
Comprehension	Vocabulary

Comprehension
— Read the following questions and statements. For each one, put an *x* in the box before the option that contains the most complete or accurate answer. Check your answers in the Answer Key on page 106.

1. How many black people die in Alabama each year for lack of proper food and nourishment?
   ☐ a. 100 ☐ c. 500
   ☐ b. 200 ☐ d. 600

2. In his letter, Rap Brown identifies as "outlaws" the members of
   ☐ a. the legislative branch of the government.
   ☐ b. the judiciary branch of the government.
   ☐ c. the executive branch of the government.
   ☐ d. all of the above.

3. The views stated in Brown's letter are
   ☐ a. archaic. ☐ c. contemporary.
   ☐ b. unrealistic. ☐ d. comparisons.

4. Brown makes clear the point that
   ☐ a. whites are helping blacks.
   ☐ b. slavery still exists in America.
   ☐ c. courts are lenient with blacks.
   ☐ d. blacks must fight for equality.

5. Brown suggests that when he was arrested in Cambridge the press
   ☐ a. treated him with respect.
   ☐ b. was not there.
   ☐ c. gave him unfair coverage.
   ☐ d. misquoted him.

6. Which of the following black leaders can best be compared to the author?
   ☐ a. Malcolm X ☐ c. Roy Wilkins
   ☐ b. Muhammad Ali ☐ d. Martin Luther King, Jr.

7. Writing the word *america* in all lowercase letters seems to be an act of
   ☐ a. carelessness.
   ☐ b. sloppiness.
   ☐ c. defiance.
   ☐ d. treason.

8. The tone of the selection is
   ☐ a. dispassionate. ☐ c. restrained.
   ☐ b. objective. ☐ d. militant.

9. Brown's personality can best be described as
   - ☐ a. apathetic.
   - ☐ b. aggressive.
   - ☐ c. humble.
   - ☐ d. complacent.

10. The author's style is
    - ☐ a. formal.
    - ☐ b. wordy.
    - ☐ c. pompous.
    - ☐ d. informal.

Study Skills, Part One—Following is a passage with blanks where words have been omitted. Next to the passage are groups of five words, one group for each blank. Complete the passage by circling the correct word for each of the blanks.

Paragraphs of Conclusion

We have been discussing the different ways that authors use paragraphs in presenting their subject and how the wise reader profits from ____(1)____ these functions.

The function of the closing paragraph is ___(2)___ : to give the reader the author's concluding remarks or ___(3)___ words on the subject. The author may do this in one of several ways.

First, although this is quite rare, the author may draw a conclusion based on the information contained in the lesson or chapter. Authors are reluctant to do this because conclusions based on an entire chapter are much too ___(4)___ to be mentioned just once at the end. We can expect to find the conclusion given early in the chapter and the facts supporting it to follow. It is likely, though, that such an important conclusion would be repeated or restated in the final paragraph.

Second, the author may use the final paragraph to ___(5)___ . Here is the opportunity to give the reader points made during the presentation one last time. In effect the author is saying, "Above all, remember this. This is what it's all been about." These summarizing remarks are most valuable to the learner and a definite aid in reviewing.

Last, the author may choose to leave the readers with one final thought—the central, all-inclusive idea around which the chapter was ___(6)___ .

You recall that when we were discussing the paragraph of introduction, we mentioned that in a sense the writer is like a speaker—using some of the same ___(7)___ in addressing an audience. Occasionally you'll find an anecdote, story, or moral used at the end as a cap to the discussion.

This is the author's last chance to reach his audience. If he wants to leave the readers with a last thought, here is where it'll be.

(1)   recognizing   repeating   accepting   restricting   organizing

(2)   misleading   revealing   significant   obvious   unclear

(3)   new   final   familiar   wise   wary

(4)   factual   interesting   entertaining   boring   important

(5)   summarize   amuse   preach   present   introduce

(6)   continued   invented   developed   instructed   reviewed

(7)   instructions   techniques   opportunities   suggestions   mannerisms

Study Skills, Part Two—Read the study skills passage again, paying special attention to the lesson being taught. Then, without looking back at the passage, complete each sentence below by writing in the missing word or words. Check the Answer Key on page 106 for the answers to Study Skills, Part One, and Study Skills, Part Two.

1. The paragraphs used by the author to finish his remarks on a subject are called paragraphs of _____ .

2. The reader can usually expect the conclusion to be given early in the chapter and the _____ supporting it to follow.

3. Summarizing remarks are a definite aid in _____ .

4. The writer is like a _____ addressing an audience.

5. The author will sometimes include an anecdote, story, or _____ to complete the discussion.

7 | What to the Slaves Is the Fourth of July?

by Frederick Douglass

Vocabulary—The five words below are from the story you are about to read. Study the words and their meanings. Then complete the ten sentences that follow, using one of the five words to fill in the blank in each sentence. Mark your answer by writing the letter of the word on the line before the sentence. Check your answers in the Answer Key on page 107.

A. perpetuate: to never stop, to continue always

B. equivocate: to use words that do not have precise meanings in order to confuse

C. conceded: acknowledged or admitted

D. responsible: able to carry out obligations, accountable for one's actions

E. sham: a pretense, a fraud

_____ 1. To a slave, the idea of freedom for all is a _____ .

_____ 2. It should be _____ by every American that slavery, in one form or another, exists throughout the United States.

_____ 3. It is a cruel _____ to ask a black man to speak in favor of liberty on the Fourth of July.

_____ 4. Douglass spoke in blunt realities and did not _____ in presenting his views.

_____ 5. That the slave is a man is an idea that has been _____ by most people.

_____ 6. If action is not taken, then the institution of slavery will continue to _____ itself.

_____ 7. It is wrong to _____ over such important issues.

_____ 8. We have a moral obligation to do what is right for the oppressed in our land—we are _____ for them.

_____ 9. A _____ being could not and would not allow such injustices to exist.

_____ 10. Once sown, the seeds of freedom will _____ , flourishing throughout future generations.

Fellow Citizens: Pardon me, and allow me to ask, why am I called upon to speak here today? What have I or those I represent to do with your national independence? Are the great principles of political freedom and of natural justice, embodied in that Declaration of Independence, extended to us? And am I, therefore, called upon to bring our humble offering to the national altar, and to confess the benefits, and express devout gratitude for the blessings resulting from your independence to us?

Would to God, both for your sakes and ours, that an affirmative answer could be truthfully returned to these questions. Then would my task be light, and my burden easy and delightful. For who is there so cold that a nation's sympathy could not warm him? Who so obdurate and dead to the claims of gratitude, that would not thankfully acknowledge such priceless benefits? Who so stolid and selfish that would not give his voice to swell the halleluiahs of a nation's jubilee, when the chains of servitude had been torn from his limbs? I am not that man. . . .

I am not included within the pale of this glorious anniversary! Your high independence only reveals the immeasurable distance between us. The blessings in which you this day rejoice are not enjoyed in common. The rich inheritance of justice, liberty, prosperity, and independence bequeathed by your fathers is shared by you, not by me. The sunlight that brought life and healing to you has brought stripes and death to me. This Fourth of July is *yours,* not *mine. You* may rejoice, *I* must mourn. To drag a man in fetters into the grand illuminated temple of liberty, and call upon him to join you in joyous anthems, were inhuman mockery and sacrilegious irony. Do you mean, citizens, to mock me, by asking me to speak today? . . .

Fellow citizens, above your national, tumultuous joy, I hear the mournful wail of millions, whose chains, heavy and grievous yesterday, are today rendered more intolerable by the jubilant shouts that reach them. If I do forget, if I do not remember those bleeding children of sorrow this day, "may my right hand forget her cunning, and may my tongue cleave to the roof of my mouth!" To forget them, to pass lightly over their wrongs, and to chime in with the popular theme, would be treason, most scandalous and shocking, and would make me a reproach before God and the world. My subject, then, fellow citizens, is "American Slavery." I shall see this day and its popular characteristics from the slave's point of view. Standing here, identified with the American bondman, making his wrongs mine, I do not hesitate to declare, with all my soul, that the character and conduct of this nation never looked blacker to me than on this Fourth of July. Whether we turn to the declarations of the past, or to the professions of the present, the conduct

Frederick Douglass, a powerful orator, delivered this address in Rochester, New York, on July 4, 1852.

of the nation seems equally hideous and revolting. America is false to the past, false to the present, and solemnly binds herself to be false to the future. Standing with God and the crushed and bleeding slave on this occasion, I will, in the name of humanity, which is outraged, in the name of liberty, which is fettered, in the name of the Constitution and the Bible, which are disregarded and trampled upon, dare to call in question and to denounce, with all the emphasis I can command, everything that serves to perpetuate slavery—the great sin and shame of America! "I will not equivocate; I will not excuse;" I will use the severest language I can command, and yet not one word shall escape me that any man, whose judgment is not blinded by prejudice, or who is not at heart a slave-holder, shall not confess to be right and just.

But I fancy I hear some of my audience say it is just in this circumstance that you and your brother Abolitionists fail to make a favorable impression on the public mind. Would you argue more and denounce less, would you persuade more and rebuke less, your cause would be much more likely to succeed. But, I submit, where all is plain there is nothing to be argued. What point in the antislavery creed would you have me argue? On what branch of the subject do the people of this country need light? Must I undertake to prove that the slave is a man? That point is conceded already. Nobody doubts it. The slaveholders themselves acknowledge it in the enactment of laws for their government. They acknowledge it when they punish disobedience on the part of the slave. There are seventy-two crimes in the State of Virginia, which, if committed by a black man (no matter how ignorant he be), subject him to the punishment of death; while only two of these same crimes will subject a white man to like punishment. What is this but the acknowledgment that the slave is a moral, intellectual, and responsible being? The manhood of the slave is conceded. It is admitted in the fact that Southern statute-books are covered with enactments, forbidding, under severe fines and penalties, the teaching of the slave to read and write. When you can point to any such laws in reference to the beasts of the field, then I may consent to argue the manhood of the slave. When the dogs in your streets, when the fowls of the air, when the cattle on your hills, when the fish of the sea, and the reptiles that crawl, shall be unable to distinguish the slave from a brute, then I will argue with you that the slave is a man!

For the present it is enough to affirm the equal manhood of the Negro race. It is not astonishing that, while we are plowing, planting, and reaping, using all kinds of mechanical tools, erecting houses, constructing bridges, building ships, working in metals of brass, iron, copper, silver, and gold; that while we are reading, writing, and cyphering, acting as clerks, mechants, and secretaries, having among us lawyers, doctors, ministers, poets, authors, editors, orators, and teachers; that while we are engaged in all the enterprises common to other men—digging gold in California, capturing the whale in the Pacific, feeding sheep and cattle on the hillside, living, moving, acting, thinking, planning, living in families as husbands, wives, and children, and above all, confessing and worshipping the Christian God, and looking hopefully for life and immortality beyond the grave—we are called upon to prove that we are men?

Would you have me argue that man is entitled to liberty? That he is the rightful owner of his own body? You have already declared it. Must I argue the wrongfulness of slavery? Is that a question for republicans? Is it to be settled by the rules of logic and argumentation, as a matter beset with great difficulty, involving a doubtful application of the principle of justice, hard to understand? How should I look today in the presence of Americans, dividing and subdividing a discourse, to show that men have a natural right to freedom, speaking of it relatively and positively, negatively and affirmatively? To do so would be to make myself ridiculous, and to offer an insult to your understanding. There is not a man beneath the canopy of heaven who does not know that slavery is wrong *for him.*

What! Am I to argue that it is wrong to make men brutes, to rob them of their liberty, to work them without wages, to keep them ignorant of their relations to their fellow men, to beat them with sticks, to flay their flesh with the lash, to load their limbs with irons, to hunt them with dogs, to sell them at auction, to sunder their families, to knock out their teeth, to burn their flesh, to starve them into obedience and submission to their masters? Must I argue that a system thus marked with blood and stained with pollution is wrong? No; I will not. I have better employment for my time and strength than such arguments would imply.

What, then, remains to be argued? Is it that slavery is not divine; that God did not establish it; that our doctors of divinity are mistaken? There is blasphemy in the thought. That which is inhuman cannot be divine. Who can reason on such a proposition? They that can, may; I cannot. The time for such argument is past.

At a time like this, scorching irony, not convincing argument, is needed. O! had I the ability, and could I reach the nation's ear, I would today pour out a fiery stream of biting ridicule, blasting reproach, withering sarcasm, and stern rebuke. For it is not light that is needed, but fire; it is not the gentle shower, but thunder. We need the

Born a slave in Maryland in 1817, Frederick Douglass escaped from bondage in 1838 and became a leading figure in the antislavery movement. He gained fame as an antislavery orator, and told his life story in three autobiographies, which he wrote at three different stages of his life.

Douglass traveled to England after the first autobiography was published in 1845. There he continued to speak against slavery and made friends who bought his freedom. Upon returning to the United States in 1847, Douglass founded the antislavery newspaper, the *North Star,* in Rochester, New York. He also discussed the problems of slavery with President Lincoln several times and served as United States minister to Haiti from 1889 to 1891. Douglass died in 1895.

storm, the whirlwind, and the earthquake. The feeling of the nation must be quickened; the conscience of the nation must be exposed; and its crimes against God and man must be denounced.

What to the American slave is your Fourth of July? I answer a day that reveals to him more than all other days of the year, the gross injustice and cruelty to which he is the constant victim. To him your celebration is a sham; your boasted liberty an unholy license; your national greatness, swelling vanity; your sounds of rejoicing are empty and heartless; your denunciation of tyrants, brass-fronted impudence; your shouts of liberty and equality, hollow mockery; your prayers and hymns, your sermons and thanksgivings, with all your religious parade and solemnity, are to him mere bombast, fraud, deception, impiety, and hypocrisy—a thin veil to cover up crimes which would disgrace a nation of savages. There is not a nation of the earth guilty of practices more shocking and bloody than are the people of these United States at this very hour.

Go where you may, search where you will, roam through all the monarchies and despotisms of the Old World, travel through South America, search out every abuse and when you have found the last, lay your facts by the side of the everyday practices of this nation, and you will say with me that, for revolting barbarity and shameless hypocrisy America reigns without a rival.

Starting Time		*Finishing Time*	
Reading Time		*Reading Rate*	
Comprehension		*Vocabulary*	

Comprehension— Read the following questions and statements. For each one, put an *x* in the box before the option that contains the most complete or accurate answer. Check your answers in the Answer Key on page 107.

1. The topic of Douglass's speech is
   - ☐ a. The Promised Land.
   - ☐ b. God's Great Promise.
   - ☐ c. American Slavery.
   - ☐ d. Freedom Lives.

2. The attitude of the slave owner toward his slaves was contradictory because he
   - ☐ a. held them accountable for their actions.
   - ☐ b. permitted them to hold church meetings.
   - ☐ c. destroyed the unity of the black family.
   - ☐ d. encouraged them to work for their freedom.

3. What type of order is this speech presented in?
   - ☐ a. ascending
   - ☐ b. chronological
   - ☐ c. historical
   - ☐ d. spatial

4. Viewed in the light of Douglass's speech, the Fourth of July celebrations can be considered
   - ☐ a. appropriate.
   - ☐ b. hypocritical.
   - ☐ c. patriotic.
   - ☐ d. artificial.

5. To Frederick Douglass, the gay, noisy Fourth of July celebrations
   - ☐ a. suggested hope for his oppressed race.
   - ☐ b. made him fear a violent slave uprising.
   - ☐ c. filled him with doubt and concern.
   - ☐ d. were cruel reminders of inhuman injustice.

6. The author's intellectualism and unique writing style is reminiscent of which modern black American?
   - ☐ a. Malcolm X
   - ☐ b. Richard Wright
   - ☐ c. H. Rap Brown
   - ☐ d. Martin Luther King, Jr.

7. Generally, the slave owners viewed their slaves in no better light than they did their animals because
   - ☐ a. they sought a moral justification for slavery.
   - ☐ b. they were morally justified as slave owners.
   - ☐ c. the American Constitution denied the slaves their human rights.
   - ☐ d. the slaves offered no resistance to their white masters.

8. The tone of the speech is one of
   - ☐ a. searching inquiry.
   - ☐ b. violent militancy.
   - ☐ c. gauche inappropriateness.
   - ☐ d. scathing indictment.

9. We can tell from this speech that Douglass is
   - ☐ a. destitute and bitter.
   - ☐ b. intelligent and angry.
   - ☐ c. egotistical and elitist.
   - ☐ d. illiterate and humble.

10. Throughout his speech, the author relies heavily on questions. They are
   - ☐ a. rhetorical.
   - ☐ b. direct.
   - ☐ c. inquisitive.
   - ☐ d. declarative.

Comprehension Skills

1. recalling specific facts	6. making a judgment
2. retaining concepts	7. making an inference
3. organizing facts	8. recognizing tone
4. understanding the main idea	9. understanding characters
5. drawing a conclusion	10. appreciation of literary forms

Study Skills, Part One—Following is a passage with blanks where words have been omitted. Next to the passage are groups of five words, one group for each blank. Complete the passage by circling the correct word for each of the blanks.

Inflexible Readers

If the reading habits of most of today's adults were to be ___(1)___ , the single adjective *inflexible* would be the most appropriate description.

To illustrate what is meant by inflexible reading, take the situation that most doctors find themselves in. All of their school years and much of their adult lives have been spent ___(2)___ vitally important material. Doctors must

(1)   approached   questioned
        described   withheld   approved

(2)   avoiding   misusing
        ignoring   questioning   studying

understand the content of textbooks and journals thoroughly. No dedicated medical practitioner is satisfied with less than 100 percent comprehension. Accordingly, medical students develop an appropriate reading skill—a thorough, slow, and careful technique leading to __(3)__ of many critically important details. The problem comes later, after medical school, when the doctor wants to settle down for an evening's enjoyment with a good novel. Most novels don't require the painstaking attention to detail that a medical text demands. But because of habits formed during years of study, the doctor has become an inflexible reader and __(4)__ intensively through whatever kind of reading material that comes to hand.

Medicine isn't the only profession that demands this technique. Lawyers, scientists, and engineers tend to read everything in the specialized way that is used to read professional texts.

Another factor leading to inflexibility can be found in the way we are first taught to read. Most of us were required to read __(5)__ from our beginning texts. By listening to us read, teachers could evaluate our __(6)__ and see how well we were learning to recognize, identify, and understand words. Our parents, too, could tell how we were doing by listening to us read.

But as beginning readers, we often learn other things at the same time: we are taught to read slowly and to pronounce words carefully, we are taught not to skip words, and we are conditioned to read in this one acceptable fashion. So, as we learn to read, the __(7)__ that will later make us inflexible readers are being established.

(3)	mastery		discovery
	progress	exposure	theory

(4)		plods		races
	skips		plots	reacts

(5)		silently		aloud
	intently		quickly	freely

(6)		attitude		poise
	interest		progress	sincerity

(7)		impressions		customs
	habits		text	studies

Study Skills, Part Two—Read the study skills passage again, paying special attention to the lesson being taught. Then, without looking back at the passage, complete each sentence below by writing in the missing word or words. Check the Answer Key on page 107 for the answers to Study Skills, Part One, and Study Skills, Part Two.

1. A word that can be used to describe the reading habits of many adults is

   _____ .

2. No dedicated doctor is satisfied with less than _____

   comprehension.

3. Many professional people tend to read everything in a _____

   way.

4. Another reason for inflexibility can be found in the way we were

   _____ to read.

5. As beginners, we are _____ to read in one acceptable fashion.

8 | # The Autobiography of Malcolm X

by Malcolm X

Vocabulary—The five words below are from the story you are about to read. Study the words and their meanings. Then complete the ten sentences that follow, using one of the five words to fill in the blank in each sentence. Mark your answer by writing the letter of the word on the line before the sentence. Check your answers in the Answer Key on page 107.

A. inevitable: unavoidable

B. propagating: spreading, disseminating

C. malignancy: an evil; a cancer

D. accomplished: proficient in a particular endeavor

E. resisted: opposed, worked against

_____ 1. Early in his career, Malcolm X was dedicated to _____ the concept that the white man was the devil.

_____ 2. Because of his violent views, Malcolm X was aware that it was _____ that he would be jailed.

_____ 3. The _____ of race prejudice in America had to be eliminated.

_____ 4. There were factions, both black and white, that _____ Malcolm's views.

_____ 5. Malcolm was _____ when it came to speaking out on racism.

_____ 6. Prejudice is not a new thing; rather, it is a _____ that has been around as long as people have.

_____ 7. Malcolm did not feel _____ in areas of academic achievement.

_____ 8. Because Malcolm X had mainly the black man's interest at heart, he felt he would always be _____ by the white man.

_____ 9. Every black person should be out _____ information on crimes against the black race.

_____ 10. When an entire race is oppressed, frustration and rebellion are _____ .

I have given to this book so much of whatever time I have because I feel, and I hope, that if I honestly and fully tell my life's account, read objectively it might prove to be a testimony of some social value.

I think that an objective reader may see how in the society to which I was exposed as a black youth here in America, for me to wind up in a prison was really just about inevitable. It happens to so many thousands of black youth.

I think that an objective reader may see how when I heard "The white man is the devil," when I played back what had been my own experiences, it was inevitable that I would respond positively; then the next twelve years of my life were devoted and dedicated to propagating that phrase among the black people.

I think, I hope, that the objective reader, in following my life—the life of only one ghetto-created Negro—may gain a better picture and understanding than he has previously had of the black ghettoes which are shaping the lives and the thinking of almost all of the 22 million Negroes who live in America.

Thicker each year in these ghettoes is the kind of teenager that I was—with the wrong kinds of heroes, and the wrong kinds of influences. I am not saying that all of them become the kind of parasite that I was. Fortunately, by far most do not. But still, the small fraction who do add up to an annual total of more and more costly, dangerous youthful criminals. The F.B.I. not long ago released a report of a shocking rise in crime each successive year since the end of World War II—ten to twelve percent each year. The report did not say so in so many words, but I am saying that the majority of that crime increase is annually spawned in the black ghettoes which the American racist society permits to exist. In the 1964 "long, hot summer" riots in major cities across the United States, the socially disinherited black ghetto youth were always at the forefront.

In this year, 1965, I am certain that more—and worse— riots are going to erupt, in yet more cities, in spite of the conscience-salving Civil Rights Bill. The reason is that the *cause* of these riots, the racist malignancy in America, has been too long unattended.

I believe that it would be almost impossible to find anywhere in America a black man who has lived further down in the mud of human society than I have; or a black man who has been any more ignorant than I have been; or a black man who has suffered more anguish during his life than I have. But it is only after the deepest darkness that the greatest light can come; it is only after extreme grief that the greatest joy can come; it is only after slavery and prison that the sweetest appreciation of freedom can come.

For the freedom of my 22 million black brothers and sisters here in America, I do believe that I have fought the best that I knew how, and the best that I could, with

In this excerpt from his autobiography, Malcolm X looks back at his life, and forward . . . to his death.

the shortcomings that I have had. I know that my shortcomings are many.

My greatest lack has been, I believe, that I don't have the kind of academic education I wish I had been able to get—to have been a lawyer, perhaps. I do believe that I might have made a good lawyer. I have always loved verbal battle, and challenge. You can believe me that if I had the time right now, I would not be one bit ashamed to go back into any New York City public school and start where I left off at the ninth grade, and go on through a degree. Because I don't begin to be academically equipped for so many of the interests that I have. For instance, I love languages. I wish I were an accomplished linguist. I don't know anything more frustrating than to be around people talking something you can't understand. Especially when they are people who look just like you. In Africa, I heard original mother tongues, such as Hausa, and Swahili, being spoken, and there I was standing like some little boy, waiting for someone to tell me what had been said; I never will forget how ignorant I felt.

Aside from the basic African dialects, I would try to learn Chinese, because it looks as if Chinese will be the most powerful political language of the future. And already I have begun studying Arabic, which I think is going to be the most powerful spiritual language of the future.

I would just like to *study.* I mean ranging study, because I have a wide-open mind. I'm interested in almost any subject you can mention. I know this is the reason I have come to really like, as individuals, some of the hosts of radio or television panel programs I have been on, and to respect their minds—because even if they have been almost steadily in disagreement with me on the race issue, they still have kept their minds open and objective about the truths of things happening in this world. Irv Kupcinet in Chicago, and Barry Farber, Barry Gray and Mike Wallace in New York—people like them. They also let me see that they respected my mind—in a way I know they never realized. The way I knew was that often they would invite my opinion on subjects off the race issue. Sometimes, after the programs, we would sit around and talk about all kinds of things, current events and other things, for an hour or more. You see, most whites, even when they credit a Negro with some intelligence, will still feel that all he can talk about is the race issue; most whites never feel that Negroes can contribute anything to other areas of thought, and ideas. You just notice how rarely you will ever hear whites asking any Negroes what they think about the problem of world health, or the space race to land men on the moon.

Every morning when I wake up, now, I regard it as having another borrowed day. In any city, wherever I go, making speeches, holding meetings of my organization, or attending to other business, black men are watching every move I make, awaiting their chance to kill me. I have said publicly many times that I know that they have their orders. Anyone who chooses not to believe what I am saying doesn't know the Muslims in the Nation of Islam.

But I am also blessed with faithful followers who are, I believe, as dedicated to me as I once was to Mr. Elijah Muhammad. Those who would hunt a man need to remember that a jungle also contains those who hunt the hunters.

I know, too, that I could suddenly die at the hands of some white racists. Or I could die at the hands of some Negro hired by the white man. Or it could be some brainwashed Negro acting on his own idea that by eliminating me he would be helping out the white man, because I talk about the white man the way I do.

Anyway, now, each day I live as if I am already dead, and I tell you what I would like for you to do. When I *am* dead—I say it that way because from the things I *know*, I do not expect to live long enough to read this book in its finished form—I want you to just watch and see if I'm not right in what I say: that the white man, in his press, is going to identify me with "hate."

He will make use of me dead, as he has made use of me alive, as a convenient symbol of "hatred"—and that will help him to escape facing the truth that all I have been doing is holding up a mirror to reflect, to show, the history of unspeakable crimes that his race has committed against my race.

You watch. I will be labeled as, at best, an "irresponsible" black man. I have always felt about this accusation that the black "leader" whom white men consider to be "responsible" is invariably the black "leader" who never gets any results. You only get action as a black man if you are regarded by the white man as "irresponsible." In fact, this much I had learned when I was just a little boy. And since I have been some kind of a "leader" of

Malcolm X was born in Omaha, Nebraska, in 1925. He lived in various places in his youth, including Milwaukee, Wisconsin, Lansing, Michigan, and Roxbury, Massachusetts. In 1946, while in Massachusetts, Malcolm X was imprisoned for burglary. In prison, he adopted the beliefs of the Black Muslims, a religious group that advocated the separation of the races. Following his release from prison, Malcolm rose through the ranks of the movement under the guidance of the prophet Elijah Muhammad. Following a disagreement with Elijah Muhammad in 1964, Malcolm X formed a rival group, the Organization of Afro-American Unity, whose aim was to attain political rights for black Americans. He also organized his own Islamic religious center, the Muslim Mosque, Inc. In 1965, before the Organization and the Mosque were firmly established, Malcolm X was assassinated at a meeting in Harlem.

black people here in the racist society of America, I have been more reassured each time the white man resisted me, or attacked me harder—because each time made me more certain that I was on the right track in the American black man's best interests. The racist white man's opposition automatically made me know that I did offer the black man something worthwhile.

Yes, I have cherished my "demagogue" role. I know that societies often have killed the people who have helped to change those societies. And if I can die having brought any light, having exposed any meaningful truth that will help to destroy the racist cancer that is malignant in the body of America—then, all of the credit is due to Allah. Only the mistakes have been mine.

Starting Time		Finishing Time	
Reading Time		Reading Rate	
Comprehension		Vocabulary	

Comprehension— Read the following questions and statements. For each one, put an *x* in the box before the option that contains the most complete or accurate answer. Check your answers in the Answer Key on page 107.

1. Which language does the author predict will be the most powerful politically?
   □ a. Russian
   □ b. Chinese
   □ c. English
   □ d. French

2. Which of the following does the author cite as a subtle form of prejudice inflicted upon black guests by television hosts?
   □ a. limiting guest's questions to racial issues
   □ b. excluding black guests from panel discussions
   □ c. diverting attention from racial issues to general subjects
   □ d. minimizing black accusations through humorous interjections

3. The author makes his point clear by
   - ☐ a. listing personal opinions.
   - ☐ b. showing cause and effect.
   - ☐ c. comparing two cultures.
   - ☐ d. introducing a time order.

4. The selection can be considered
   - ☐ a. a justification of Malcolm's life and convictions.
   - ☐ b. the final document of a man who has fought well but lost.
   - ☐ c. autobiographical, and therefore lacking in objectivity.
   - ☐ d. the work of a demagogue.

5. We can conclude from the selection that Malcolm X
   - ☐ a. was born in the South.
   - ☐ b. could never hold a decent job.
   - ☐ c. believed in peaceful change.
   - ☐ d. did not have a high school diploma.

6. Which of the following black leaders used an approach similar to Malcolm's?
   - ☐ a. Dr. Martin Luther King, Jr.
   - ☐ b. George Washington Carver
   - ☐ c. H. Rap Brown
   - ☐ d. Bill Cosby

7. "Those who would hunt a man need to remember that a jungle also contains those who hunt the hunters." That statement can be considered a
   - ☐ a. promise.
   - ☐ c. challenge.
   - ☐ b. surrender.
   - ☐ d. warning.

8. The tone of this selection shows
   - ☐ a. humor.
   - ☐ c. resignation.
   - ☐ b. anger.
   - ☐ d. sarcasm.

9. From the details Malcolm X reveals about his own background, one is impressed by his
   - ☐ a. lack of personal objectivity.
   - ☐ b. lack of foresight in the face of danger.
   - ☐ c. humble, candid, and frank admissions.
   - ☐ d. rise to prominence in spite of his illiteracy.

10. This selection presents
   - ☐ a. numerical facts.
   - ☐ c. puzzling parables.
   - ☐ b. a fictitious story.
   - ☐ d. biographical data.

Comprehension Skills

1. recalling specific facts	6. making a judgment
2. retaining concepts	7. making an inference
3. organizing facts	8. recognizing tone
4. understanding the main idea	9. understanding characters
5. drawing a conclusion	10. appreciation of literary forms

Study Skills, Part One—Following is a passage with blanks where words have been omitted. Next to the passage are groups of five words, one group for each blank. Complete the passage by circling the correct word for each of the blanks.

Flexible Reading

A good reader is flexible. His reading technique is varied to suit the occasion. He knows that there are many kinds of reading and tries to become ___(1)___ in all of them. Some materials demand a slow, ___(2)___ approach; insurance policies and contracts are good examples. Light fiction calls for a breezy, casual kind of reading at a fairly rapid rate. Another kind of material permits the reader to quickly glance down the column of print, snatching ideas on the run. This is called ___(3)___ . Let us examine the kind of material it is appropriate for.

SUITABLE MATERIAL

We often run across articles, accounts, and stories that are of just ___(4)___ or passing interest to us. These may be unrelated to school or the job; they may contain very little factual content; and they are very simply written. To read these materials analytically like contracts and documents would be a waste of time. To use our study skills and

(1)	useful	skilled
	interested	involved	responsible

(2)	analytical	thoughtless
	cautious	considerate	conservative

(3)	cheating	plotting
	skimming	practicing	reviewing

(4)	important	unusual
	great	beneficial	casual

techniques on them would be ___(5)___ and wasted effort. These materials need only to be skimmed to be ___(6)___ .

COMPREHENSION LEVEL

Comprehension is another aspect of flexible reading. There are degrees or levels of comprehension which are ___(7)___ for certain materials. For example, a very practical and thorough kind is needed to follow directions accurately. Obviously we don't need this for reading the comics. Textbooks require the student to remember concepts and to understand relationships. The student, moreover, is expected to use comprehension as a tool for thinking. But simple articles of passing interest require only a temporary kind of comprehension—the kind that comes from skimming.

(5) appropriate   unwise
     useful   nonproductive   unfortunate

(6) appreciated   misunderstood
     comprehended   avoided   analyzed

(7) appropriate   apparent
     unnecessary   unusual   unrelated

Study Skills, Part Two—Read the study skills passage again, paying special attention to the lesson being taught. Then, without looking back at the passage, complete each sentence below by writing in the missing word or words. Check the Answer Key on page 107 for the answers to Study Skills, Part One, and Study Skills, Part Two.

1. A good reader _____ his reading technique to suit the occasion.

2. Some materials such as insurance policies and contracts must be read at

   a _____ rate in order to be understood.

3. Light fiction calls for an informal kind of reading at a fairly

   _____ rate.

4. Textbooks require the student to remember _____ and

   understand relationships.

5. Simple articles require only a temporary kind of comprehension, the kind

   that comes from _____ .

9 | # The Color Purple

by Alice Walker

Vocabulary—The five words below are from the story you are about to read. Study the words and their meanings. Then complete the ten sentences that follow, using one of the five words to fill in the blank in each sentence. Mark your answer by writing the letter of the word on the line before the sentence. Check your answers in the Answer Key on page 107.

A. fell through: was unsuccessful, failed

B. slaving: working hard

C. affliction: the cause of suffering or distress

D. flustered: emotionally upset; agitated

E. frustrate: to defeat in an endeavor

_____ 1. Sofia's shortened visit to her children was enough to _____ a saint.

_____ 2. As the gears on the car became stripped, Miz Millie became more and more _____ .

_____ 3. The people Sofia worked for could be described as her _____ .

_____ 4. It could be said that Sofia's plans to spend the day with her children _____ .

_____ 5. Sofia could be found any time of the day, _____ away.

_____ 6. Working as a slave for white folks began to _____ Sofia.

_____ 7. Poverty has always been an _____ of blacks in America.

_____ 8. Seeing the mistress all _____ was an amusing sight.

_____ 9. The servant's duties included _____ over a hot stove in the kitchen.

_____ 10. Because many black children were needed at home to work, ideas about finishing school often _____ .

Dear God,

Sofia would make a dog laugh, talking about those people she work for. They have the nerve to try to make us think slavery fell through because of us, say Sofia. Like us didn't have sense enough to handle it. All the time breaking hoe handles and letting the mules loose in the wheat. But how anything they build can last a day is a wonder to me. They backward, she say. Clumsy, and unlucky.

Mayor _____ bought Miz Millie a new car, cause she said if colored could have cars then one for her was past due. So he bought her a car, only he refuse to show her how to drive it. Every day he come home from town he look at her, look out the window at her car, say, How you enjoying 'er Miz Millie. She fly off the sofa in a huff, slam the door going in the bathroom.

She ain't got no friends.

So one day she say to me, car been sitting out in the yard two months, Sofia, do you know how to drive? I guess she remembered first seeing me up gainst Buster Broadnax car.

Yes ma'am, I say. I'm slaving away cleaning that big post they got down at the bottom of the stair. They act real funny bout that post. No finger prints is sposed to be on it, ever.

Do you think you could teach me? she says.

One of Sofia children break in, the oldest boy. He tall and handsome, all the time serious. And mad a lot.

He say, Don't say slaving, Mama.

Sofia say, Why not? They got me in a little storeroom up under the house, hardly bigger than Odessa's porch, and just about as warm in the winter time. I'm at they beck and call all night and all day. They won't let me see my children. They won't let me see no mens. Well, after five years they let me see you once a year. I'm a slave, she say. What would you call it?

A captive, he say.

Sofia go on with her story, only look at him like she glad he hers.

So I say, Yes ma'am. I can teach you, if it the same kind of car I learned on.

Next thing you know there go me and Miz Millie all up and down the road. First I drive and she watch, then she start to try to drive and I watch her. Up and down the road. Soon as I finish cooking breakfast, putting it on the table, washing dishes and sweeping the floor— and just before I go git the mail out of the box down by the road—we go give Miz Millie her driving lesson.

Well, after while she got the hang of it, more or less. Then she really git it. Then one day when we come home from riding, she say to me, I'm gonna drive you home. Just like that.

Home? I ast.

Yes, she say. Home. You ain't been home or seen your

For teaching Miz Millie to drive, Sofia's reward was a maddening episode that left her lonelier than ever.

children in a while, she say. Ain't that right?

I say, Yes ma'am. It been five years.

She say, That's a shame. You just go git your things right now. Here it is, Christmas. Go get your things. You can stay all day.

For all day I don't need nothing but what I got on, I say.

Fine, she say. Fine. Well git in.

Well, say Sofia, I was so use to sitting up there next to her teaching her how to drive, that I just naturally clammed into the front seat.

She stood outside on her side the car clearing her throat.

Finally she say, Sofia, with a little laugh, This *is* the South.

Yes ma'am, I say.

She clear her throat, laugh some more. Look where you sitting, she say.

I'm sitting where I always sit, I say.

That's the problem, she say. Have you ever seen a white person and a colored sitting side by side in a car, when one of 'em wasn't showing the other one how to drive it or clean it?

I got out the car, opened the back door and clammed in. She sat down up front. Off us traveled down the road, Miz Millie hair blowing all out the window.

It's real pretty country out this way, she say, when we hit the Marshall county road, coming toward Odessa's house.

Yes ma'am, I say.

Then us pull into the yard and all the children come crowding round the car. Nobody told them I was coming, so they don't know who I is. Except the oldest two. They fall on me, and hug me. And then all the little ones start to hug me too. I don't think they even notice I was sitting in the back of the car. Odessa and Jack come out after I was out, so they didn't see it.

Us all stand round kissing and hugging each other, Miz Millie just watching. Finally, she lean out the window and say, Sofia, you only got the rest of the day. I'll be back to pick you up at five o'clock. The children was all pulling me into the house, so sort of over my shoulder I say, Yes ma'am, and I thought I heard her drive off.

But fifteen minutes later, Marion says, That white lady still out there.

Maybe she going to wait to take you back, say Jack.

Maybe she sick, say Odessa. You always say how sickly they is.

I go out to the car, say Sofia, and guess what the matter is? The matter is, she don't know how to do nothing but go forward, and Jack and Odessa's yard too full of trees for that.

Sofia, she say, How you back this thing up?

I lean over the car window and try to show her which way to move the gears. But she flustered and all the children and Odessa and Jack all standing round the porch watching her.

I go round on the other side. Try to explain with my head poked through that window. She stripping gears aplenty by now. Plus her nose red and she look mad and frustrate both.

I clam in the back seat, lean over the back of the front, steady trying to show her how to operate the gears. Nothing happen. Finally the car stop making any sound. Engine dead.

Don't worry, I say, Odessa's husband Jack will drive you home. That's his pick-up right there.

Oh, she say, I couldn't ride in a pick-up with a strange colored man.

I'll ask Odessa to squeeze in too, I say. That would give me a chance to spend a little time with the children, I thought. But she say, No, I don't know her neither.

So it end up with me and Jack driving her back home in the pick-up, then Jack driving me to town to git a mechanic, and at five o'clock I was driving Miz Millie's car back to her house.

I spent fifteen minutes with my children.

And she been going on for months bout how ungrateful I is.

White folks is a miracle of affliction, say Sofia.

Best known for her highly acclaimed third novel *The Color Purple*, Alice Walker has also written volumes of short stories and poems. Themes of racism and sexism are predominant in Walker's work and her central characters are generally black women.

Walker received the Pulitzer Prize and the American Book Award in 1983 for *The Color Purple*. She received the Guggenheim Award in 1977, was nominated for the National Book Critics Circle Award in 1982, and has received various writing fellowships. Walker resides in San Francisco, California.

Starting Time		*Finishing Time*	
Reading Time		*Reading Rate*	
Comprehension		*Vocabulary*	

Comprehension

Comprehension— Read the following questions and statements. For each one, put an *x* in the box before the option that contains the most complete or accurate answer. Check your answers in the Answer Key on page 107.

1. Who drove Miz Millie and Sofia to town?
   - ☐ a. Jack
   - ☐ b. Odessa
   - ☐ c. Marion
   - ☐ d. Millie

2. Sofia thought that white folks were
   - ☐ a. thrifty.
   - ☐ b. humorous.
   - ☐ c. stupid.
   - ☐ d. cocky.

3. The facts in this story are presented in the order
   - ☐ a. of importance.
   - ☐ b. of spatial arrangements.
   - ☐ c. of a number statement.
   - ☐ d. in which they happened.

4. According to Sofia, a servant is nothing more than
   - ☐ a. an immigrant.
   - ☐ b. a slave.
   - ☐ c. an apprentice.
   - ☐ d. an intern.

5. This story takes place during the
   - ☐ a. summer.
   - ☐ b. fall.
   - ☐ c. winter.
   - ☐ d. spring.

6. Miz Millie made Sofia sit in the back seat of the car because she
   - ☐ a. could not stand the sight of Sofia.
   - ☐ b. wanted to make Sofia feel important.
   - ☐ c. believed in keeping the races separate.
   - ☐ d. could get a better view of the road.

7. Miz Millie's husband was
   - ☐ a. a teacher.
   - ☐ b. an inventor.
   - ☐ c. a writer.
   - ☐ d. a politician.

8. The tone of the selection is
   - ☐ a. depressing.
   - ☐ b. humorous.
   - ☐ c. nostalgic.
   - ☐ d. aggressive.

9. Miz Millie shows herself to be
   - ☐ a. unintelligent.
   - ☐ b. defiant.
   - ☐ c. self-important.
   - ☐ d. sarcastic.

10. This story is presented in the form of
- ☐ a. an apology.
- ☐ b. a fable.
- ☐ c. a thesis.
- ☐ d. a letter.

Study Skills, Part One—Following is a passage with blanks where words have been omitted. Next to the passage are groups of five words, one group for each blank. Complete the passage by circling the correct word for each of the blanks.

Skimming for Facts

Skimming is an art and a skill—it is not careless reading.

STUDY-TYPE MATERIAL

Another kind of material that permits the reader to skim is study-type matter in which the student wishes to locate certain facts or extract __(1)__ data. Actually this is a reference skill—skimming through a chapter or lesson to see if a particular topic is discussed or covered. When the student finds what he is looking for, other reading and study techniques can be __(2)__ . Consider this type of skimming a more thorough kind of previewing.

When skimming for facts, here is how to proceed.

1. Read the Title. This may tell you if the author's subject is one that might include your __(3)__ .

2. Read the Subhead. Be alert for a word pertaining to your topic. See if the author announces a category or classification that might include it.

3. Read the Illustration. Look for __(4)__ information relating to what you are seeking.

4. Read First Sentences. Look for paragraphs that contain information and definitions. These are the ones most likely to contain __(5)__ data. Skim through these looking for your topic. __(6)__ of introduction may tell you that what you are seeking is coming next. Paragraphs of illustration will probably not contain factual data— these may be glossed over or __(7)__ entirely. The closing paragraph is not likely to help, either.

Skimming for facts is a valuable reference skill and one more tool of the flexible reader.

(1)
| unusual | | specific |
| unimportant | trivial | meaningless |

(2)
| employed | | eliminated |
| enjoyed | reviewed | rejected |

(3)
| interest | | opinions |
| ideas | information | technique |

(4)
| grammatic | | inconsistent |
| graphic | insignificant | general |

(5)
| factual | | erroneous |
| frequent | fictional | technical |

(6)
| Statements | | Indexes |
| Paragraphs | Chapters | Books |

(7)
| reread | | studied |
| comprehended | reviewed | skipped |

Study Skills, Part Two—Read the study skills passage again, paying special attention to the lesson being taught. Then, without looking back at the passage, complete each sentence below by writing in the missing word or words. Check the Answer Key on page 107 for the answers to Study Skills, Part One, and Study Skills, Part Two.

1. Skimming is an art and a skill—it is not _____ reading.

2. Another kind of material that permits the reader to skim is

   _____ matter in which the student locates certain facts.

3. Reading the _____ may tell you if the author's subject includes

   information that you need.

4. Look for paragraphs that contain information and _____ .

5. Skimming for facts is a valuable _____ skill.

Sula, I

by Toni Morrison

Vocabulary—The five words below are from the story you are about to read. Study the words and their meanings. Then complete the ten sentences that follow, using one of the five words to fill in the blank in each sentence. Mark your answer by writing the letter of the word on the line before the sentence. Check your answers in the Answer Key on page 107.

A. fastidious: very proper, straightlaced

B. repugnance: dislike or distaste

C. equilibrium: balance

D. ruefully: mournfully

E. guffaw: a loud laugh

_____ 1. The odor of the food before Shadrack made him wince with _____ .

_____ 2. The ground shook with the explosions, causing each soldier to question his sense of _____ .

_____ 3. Shadrack _____ looked about the sterile walls, looking for something familiar.

_____ 4. Even the most _____ citizens of the town could not help but pity the poor, demented soul.

_____ 5. Shadrack teetered on the top landing, trying to regain the _____ he had lost through too many days in bed.

_____ 6. It seemed ironic, but somewhere on the battlefield a type of insane _____ could be heard.

_____ 7. Shadrack was filled with _____ when he recalled that day on the battlefield.

_____ 8. Again and again the _____ of the deranged patient was heard throughout the hospital.

_____ 9. The chaos of war disturbed those soldiers with _____ personalities.

_____ 10. Almost _____ , the orderly closed the heavy door behind Shadrack as he slept.

Except for World War II, nothing ever interfered with the celebration of National Suicide Day. It had taken place every January third since 1920, although Shadrack, its founder, was for many years the only celebrant. Blasted and permanently astonished by the events of 1917, he had returned to Medallion handsome but ravaged, and even the most fastidious people in the town sometimes caught themselves dreaming of what he must have been like a few years back before he went off to war. A young man of hardly twenty, his head full of nothing and his mouth recalling the taste of lipstick, Shadrack had found himself in December, 1917, running with his comrades across a field in France. It was his first encounter with the enemy and he didn't know whether his company was running toward them or away. For several days they had been marching, keeping close to a stream that was frozen at its edges. At one point they crossed it, and no sooner had he stepped foot on the other side than the day was adangle with shouts and explosions. Shellfire was all around him, and though he knew that this was something called *it,* he could not muster up the proper feeling—the feeling that would accommodate *it.* He expected to be terrified or exhilarated—to feel *something* very strong. In fact, he felt only the bite of a nail in his boot, which pierced the ball of his foot whenever he came down on it. The day was cold enough to make his breath visible, and he wondered for a moment at the purity and whiteness of his own breath among the dirty, gray explosions surrounding him. He ran, bayonet fixed, deep in the great sweep of men flying across this field. Wincing at the pain in his foot, he turned his head a little to the right and saw the face of a soldier near him fly off. Before he could register shock, the rest of the soldier's head disappeared under the inverted soup bowl of his helmet. But stubbornly, taking no direction from the brain, the body of the headless soldier ran on, with energy and grace, ignoring altogether the drip and slide of brain tissue down its back.

When Shadrack opened his eyes he was propped up in a small bed. Before him on a tray was a large tin plate divided into three triangles. In one triangle was rice, in another meat, and in the third stewed tomatoes. A small round depression held a cup of whitish liquid. Shadrack stared at the soft colors that filled these triangles: the lumpy whiteness of rice, the quivering blood tomatoes, the grayish-brown meat. All their repugnance was contained in the neat balance of the triangles—a balance that soothed him, transferred some of its equilibrium to him. Thus reassured that the white, the red and the brown would stay where they were—would not explode or burst forth from their restricted zones—he suddenly felt hungry and looked around for his hands. His glance was cautious at first, for he had to be very careful—anything could be anywhere. Then he noticed two lumps beneath the

For some soldiers there is ease at the end of war. For Shadrack there was no end, no ease.

beige blanket on either side of his hips. With extreme care he lifted one arm and was relieved to find his hand attached to his wrist. He tried the other and found it also. Slowly he directed one hand toward the cup and, just as he was about to spread his fingers, they began to grow in higgledy-piggledy fashion like Jack's beanstalk all over the tray and the bed. With a shriek he closed his eyes and thrust his huge growing hands under the covers. Once out of sight they seemed to shrink back to their normal size. But the yell had brought a male nurse.

"Private? We're not going to have any trouble today, are we? Are we, Private?"

Shadrack looked up at the balding man dressed in a green-cotton jacket and trousers. His hair was parted low on the right side so that some twenty or thirty yellow hairs could discreetly cover the nakedness of his head.

"Come on. Pick up that spoon. Pick it up, Private. Nobody is going to feed you forever."

Sweat slid from Shadrack's armpits down his sides. He could not bear to see his hands grow again and he was frightened of the voice in the apple-green suit.

"Pick it up, I said. There's no point to this . . ." The nurse reached under the cover for Shadrack's wrist to pull out the monstrous hand. Shadrack jerked it back and overturned the tray. In panic he raised himself to his knees and tried to fling off and away his terrible fingers, but succeeded only in knocking the nurse into the next bed.

When they bound Shadrack into a straitjacket, he was both relieved and grateful, for his hands were at last hidden and confined to whatever size they had attained.

Laced and silent in his small bed, he tried to tie the loose cords in his mind. He wanted desperately to see his own face and connect it with the word "private"— the word the nurse (and the others who helped bind him) had called him. "Private" he thought was something secret, and he wondered why they looked at him and called him a secret. Still, if his hands behaved as they had done, what might he expect from his face? The fear and longing were too much for him, so he began to think of other things. That is, he let his mind slip into whatever cave mouths of memory it chose.

He saw a window that looked out on a river which he knew was full of fish. Someone was speaking softly just outside the door . . .

Shadrack's earlier violence had coincided with a memorandum from the hospital executive staff in reference to the distribution of patients in high-risk areas. There was clearly a demand for space. The priority or the violence earned Shadrack his release, $217 in cash, a full suit of clothes and copies of very official-looking papers.

When he stepped out of the hospital door the grounds

overwhelmed him: the cropped shrubbery, the edged lawns, the undeviating walks. Shadrack looked at the cement stretches: each one leading clearheadedly to some presumably desirable destination. There were no fences, no warnings, no obstacles at all between concrete and green grass, so one could easily ignore the tidy sweep of stone and cut out in another direction—a direction of one's own.

Shadrack stood at the foot of the hospital steps watching the heads of trees tossing ruefully but harmlessly, since their trunks were rooted too deeply in the earth to threaten him. Only the walks made him uneasy. He shifted his weight, wondering how he could get to the gate without stepping on the concrete. While plotting his course—where he would have to leap, where to skirt a clump of bushes—a loud guffaw startled him. Two men were going up the steps. Then he noticed that there were many people about, and that he was just now seeing them, or else they had just materialized. They were thin slips, like paper dolls floating down the walks. Some were seated in chairs with wheels, propelled by other paper figures from behind. All seemed to be smoking, and their arms and legs curved in the breeze. A good high wind would pull them up and away and they would land perhaps among the tops of the trees.

Shadrack took the plunge. Four steps and he was on the grass heading for the gate. He kept his head down to avoid seeing the paper people swerving and bending here and there, and he lost his way. When he looked up, he was standing by a low red building separated from the main building by a covered walkway. From somewhere came a sweetish smell which reminded him of something painful. He looked around for the gate and saw that he had gone directly away from it in his complicated journey over the grass. Just to the left of the low building was a graveled driveway that appeared to lead outside the grounds. He trotted quickly to it and left, at last, a haven of more than a year, only eight days of which he fully recollected.

Toni Morrison was born in Lorain, Ohio, in 1931. She graduated from Howard University and received her master's degree from Cornell University. Morrison taught English at Texas Southern University and Howard University. She has been a senior editor at Random House, New York, and visiting lecturer at Yale University.

Morrison's novels include *The Bluest Eye, Song of Solomon* (winner of the 1978 National Book Critics Circle Award), and *Sula*, among others.

Starting Time		Finishing Time	
Reading Time		Reading Rate	
Comprehension		Vocabulary	

Comprehension— Read the following questions and statements. For each one, put an *x* in the box before the option that contains the most complete or accurate answer. Check your answers in the Answer Key on page 107.

1. Shadrack lived in the city of
   ☐ a. Medallion.
   ☐ b. Valentine.
   ☐ c. Meadowview.
   ☐ d. Stockton.

2. Shadrack's disability could be classified as
   ☐ a. mortal.
   ☐ b. psychiatric.
   ☐ c. cardiac.
   ☐ d. pediatric.

3. The facts in this passage are presented
   ☐ a. as a spatial development.
   ☐ b. in a simple list.
   ☐ c. as alphabetical indexes.
   ☐ d. to show cause and effect.

4. Which of the following titles best fits the selection?
   ☐ a. A Reason to Die
   ☐ b. Invisible Wounds
   ☐ c. Overcoming the Enemy
   ☐ d. A Place to Live

5. Shadrack fought in
   ☐ a. World War I.
   ☐ b. World War II.
   ☐ c. Korea.
   ☐ d. Vietnam.

6. When Shadrack left the hospital he was
   ☐ a. elated.
   ☐ b. melancholy.
   ☐ c. unprepared.
   ☐ d. organized.

7. Shadrack's feelings on the day of his first encounter with the enemy bordered on
   ☐ a. humor.
   ☐ b. terror.
   ☐ c. apathy.
   ☐ d. concern.

8. After reading this selection, one is left with an overall feeling of
   ☐ a. anger.
   ☐ b. contentment.
   ☐ c. pity.
   ☐ d. elation.

9. The last quality Shadrack exhibits in this selection is one of
   ☐ a. enjoyment.   ☐ c. ignorance.
   ☐ b. courage.   ☐ d. understanding.

10. The reference to "Jack's beanstalk" makes use of
   ☐ a. alliteration. ☐ c. onomatopeia.
   ☐ b. a contrast.   ☐ d. a simile.

Study Skills, Part One—Following is a passage with blanks where words have been omitted. Next to the passage are groups of five words, one group for each blank. Complete the passage by circling the correct word for each of the blanks.

Dynamic Skimming

We can label another type of high speed skimming dynamic skimming. We call it dynamic because of the ___(1)___ results it yields at such high speeds. You may have seen demonstrations of this type of reading on television or have read about it somewhere. The fact that some reading courses charge fees close to two hundred dollars testifies to the ___(2)___ of this kind of reading as a tool in the repertory of the flexible reader. The steps to dynamic skimming are these.

1. Preview. As you no doubt have begun to realize, previewing is ___(3)___ to reading of any kind. In dynamic skimming, previewing is more essential than ever. Before skimming, the reader must ___(4)___ a thorough and comprehensive preview of the entire article. The steps to previewing do not change. It's just that more time is spent on previewing to form a clear mental outline of the article for skimming.

2. Skim. This time let your eyes flow down the column of print, snatching ideas on the run. Do not stop to read—do not pause to reflect. Strive to let the words ___(5)___ your mind as you skim by.

This kind of skimming is ___(6)___ at first because we've been in the habit of reading line by line. To overcome this natural tendency, use your finger as a pacer to force your eyes down the page. You may wish to move your finger in a zigzag fashion, letting the eyes fixate (stop and read) twice on each line. Gradually speed up until you are able to cover the page in ten or twelve seconds.

3. Reread. This is the third step to dynamic skimming. Rereading is done like previewing, attempting to ___(7)___ any gaps in your understanding of the article.

To be successful, you must have easy material and perform each of the three steps: preview, skim, and reread.

(1)   poor   negligible
   impressive   knowledgeable   minimal

(2)   value   fact
       concept   root   bond

(3)   unwise   optional
   prohibitive   preferable   necessary

(4)   study   perform
   review   predict   anticipate

(5)   trigger   leave
   absorb   open   possess

(6)   necessary   trivial
   difficult   boring   unusual

(7)   read   enjoy
       study   fill   scan

Study Skills, Part Two—Read the study skills passage again, paying special attention to the lesson being taught. Then, without looking back at the passage, complete each sentence below by writing in the missing word or words. Check the Answer Key on page 107 for the answers to Study Skills, Part One, and Study Skills, Part Two.

1. High speed skimming is called _____ skimming.

2. _____ is necessary for reading of any kind.

3. While skimming, your eyes flow down the column of print snatching

   _____ on the run.

4. _____ is the third step to dynamic skimming.

5. To be successful in the art of skimming, you must have _____

   material.

11 | Sula, II

by Toni Morrison

Vocabulary—The five words below are from the story you are about to read. Study the words and their meanings. Then complete the ten sentences that follow, using one of the five words to fill in the blank in each sentence. Mark your answer by writing the letter of the word on the line before the sentence. Check your answers in the Answer Key on page 107.

A. manipulation: doing things with one's hands

B. abated: subsided; eased

C. unequivocal: clear, precise, and direct

D. skittish: nervous

E. goading: teasing to bring about action

_____ 1. Some of the local rowdies would start _____ Shadrack as he paraded down the street.

_____ 2. After so many years of confinement, even the simplest _____ was a grueling task.

_____ 3. Frail, _____ visions of past events played at the edge of Shadrack's mind.

_____ 4. With an _____ clarity, the black man's place in Medallion was defined.

_____ 5. After a while, people realized the nature of the poor man's illness and all _____ stopped.

_____ 6. Looking at the entangled bootlaces, the policeman wondered at Shadrack's lack of the powers of _____ .

_____ 7. The first National Suicide Day left the people of Medallion with an uneasy, _____ feeling.

_____ 8. The fiery liquid _____ much of the apprehension Shadrack felt.

_____ 9. It was an _____ fact of life that Shadrack was possessed of some sort of madness.

_____ 10. The young man's agony over the events of the day slowly _____ as sleep overtook him.

Once on the road, he headed west. The long stay in the hospital had left him weak—too weak to walk steadily on the gravel shoulders of the road. He shuffled, grew dizzy, stopped for breath, started again, stumbling and sweating but refusing to wipe his temples, still afraid to look at his hands. Passengers in dark, square cars shuttered their eyes at what they took to be a drunken man.

The sun was already directly over his head when he came to a town. A few blocks of shaded streets and he was already at its heart—a pretty, quietly regulated downtown.

Exhausted, his feet clotted with pain, he sat down at the curbside to take off his shoes. He closed his eyes to avoid seeing his hands and fumbled with the laces of the heavy high-topped shoes. The nurse had tied them into a double knot, the way one does for children, and Shadrack, long unaccustomed to the manipulation of intricate things, could not get them loose. Uncoordinated, his fingernails tore away at the knots. He fought a rising hysteria that was not merely anxiety to free his aching feet; his very life depended on the release of the knots. Suddenly without raising his eyelids, he began to cry. Twenty-two years old, weak, hot, frightened, not daring to acknowledge the fact that he didn't even know who or what he was . . . with no past, no language, no tribe, no source, no address book, no comb, no pencil, no clock, no pocket handkerchief, no rug, no bed, no can opener, no faded postcard, no soap, no key, no tobacco pouch, no soiled underwear and nothing nothing nothing to do . . . he was sure of one thing only: the unchecked monstrosity of his hands. He cried soundlessly at the curbside of a small Midwestern town wondering where the window was, and the river, and the soft voices just outside the door . . .

Through his tears he saw the fingers joining the laces, tentatively at first, then rapidly. The four fingers of each hand fused into the fabric, knotted themselves and zig-zagged in and out of the tiny eyeholes.

By the time the police drove up, Shadrack was suffering from a blinding headache, which was not abated by the comfort he felt when the policemen pulled his hands away from what he thought was a permanent entanglement with his shoelaces. They took him to jail, booked him for vagrancy and intoxication, and locked him in a cell. Lying on a cot, Shadrack could only stare helplessly at the wall, so paralyzing was the pain in his head. He lay in this agony for a long while and then realized he was staring at the painted-over letters of a command to fuck himself. He studied the phrase as the pain in his head subsided.

Like moonlight stealing under a window shade an idea insinuated itself: his earlier desire to see his own face. He looked for a mirror; there was none. Finally, keeping his hands carefully behind his back he made his way to the toilet bowl and peeped in. The water was unevenly lit by the sun so he could make nothing out. Returning to his cot he took the blanket and covered his head, rendering the water dark enough to see his reflection. There in the toilet water he saw a grave black face. A black so definite, so unequivocal, it astonished him. He had been harboring a skittish apprehension that he was not real—that he didn't exist at all. But when the blackness greeted him with its indisputable presence, he wanted nothing more. In his joy he took the risk of letting one edge of the blanket drop and glanced at his hands. They were still. Courteously still.

Shadrack rose and returned to the cot, where he fell into the first sleep of his new life. A sleep deeper than the hospital drugs; deeper than the pits of plums, steadier than the condor's wing; more tranquil than the curve of eggs.

The sheriff looked through the bars at the young man with the matted hair. He had read through his prisoner's papers and hailed a farmer. When Shadrack awoke, the sheriff handed him back his papers and escorted him to the back of a wagon. Shadrack got in and in less than three hours he was back in Medallion, for he had been only twenty-two miles from his window, his river, and his soft voices just outside the door.

In the back of the wagon, supported by sacks of squash and hills of pumpkins, Shadrack began a struggle that was to last for twelve days, a struggle to order and focus experience. It had to do with making a place for fear as a way of controlling it. He knew the smell of death and was terrified of it, for he could not anticipate it. It was not death or dying that frightened him, but the unexpectedness of both. In sorting it all out, he hit on the notion that if one day a year were devoted to it, everybody could get it out of the way and the rest of the year would be safe and free. In this manner he instituted National Suicide Day.

On the third day of the new year, he walked through the Bottom down Carpenter's Road with a cowbell and a hangman's rope calling the people together. Telling them that this was their only chance to kill themselves or each other.

At first the people in the town were frightened; they knew Shadrack was crazy but that did not mean that he didn't have any sense or, even more important, that he had no power. His eyes were so wild, his hair so long and matted, his voice was so full of authority and thunder that he caused panic on the first, or Charter, National Suicide Day in 1920. The next one, in 1921, was less frightening but still worrisome. The people had seen him a year now in between. He lived in a shack on the riverbank that had once belonged to his grandfather long time dead. On Tuesday and Friday he sold the fish he had caught that morning, the rest of the week he was drunk, loud, obscene, funny and outrageous. But he never touched anybody, never fought, never caressed. Once the people understood the boundaries and nature of

> Shadrack eventually struck an uneasy peace with oblivion—one day each year devoted to death, the rest to life, safe and happy.

his madness, they could fit him, so to speak, into the scheme of things.

Then, on subsequent National Suicide Days, the grown people looked out from behind curtains as he rang his bell; a few stragglers increased their speed, and little children screamed and ran. The tetter heads tried goading him (although he was only four or five years older then they) but not for long, for his curses were stingingly personal.

As time went along, the people took less notice of these January thirds, or rather they thought they did, thought they had no attitudes or feelings one way or another about Shadrack's annual solitary parade. In fact they had simply stopped remarking on the holiday because they had absorbed it into their thoughts, into their language, into their lives.

Someone said to a friend, "You sure was a long time delivering that baby. How long was you in labor?"

And the friend answered, " 'Bout three days. The pains started on Suicide Day and kept up till the following Sunday. Was borned on Sunday. All my boys is Sunday boys."

Some lover said to his bride-to-be, "Let's do it after New Years, 'stead of before. I get paid New Year's Eve."

And his sweetheart answered, "OK, but make sure it ain't on Suicide Day. I ain't 'bout to be listening to no cowbells whilst the weddin's going on."

Somebody's grandmother said her hens always started a laying of double yolks right after Suicide Day.

Then Reverend Deal took it up, saying the same folks who had sense enough to avoid Shadrack's call were the ones who insisted on drinking themselves to death or womanizing themselves to death. "May's well go on with Shad and save the Lamb the trouble of redemption."

Easily, quietly, Suicide Day became a part of the fabric of life up in the Bottom of Medallion, Ohio.

Starting Time		Finishing Time	
Reading Time		Reading Rate	
Comprehension		Vocabulary	

Comprehension— Read the following questions and statements. For each one, put an x in the box before the option that contains the most complete or accurate answer. Check your answers in the Answer Key on page 107.

1. The first National Suicide Day took place in
   □ a. 1919.
   □ b. 1920.
   □ c. 1921.
   □ d. 1922.

2. As the years went on, the attitude of the people in Medallion toward Shadrack went from
   □ a. love to hate.
   □ b. apathy to action.
   □ c. acceptance to indifference.
   □ d. fright to tolerance.

3. The facts in this story are arranged in
   □ a. chronological order.
   □ b. spatial order.
   □ c. order of importance.
   □ d. ascending order.

4. Suicide Day was Shadrack's way of
   □ a. honoring all dead soldiers.
   □ b. dealing with death.
   □ c. solving the effects of war.
   □ d. rejecting the white population.

5. We can assume that Shadrack was from the
   □ a. Northeast.   □ c. Midwest.
   □ b. deep South.   □ d. West.

6. It could be said that Shadrack was
   □ a. accepted by the community.
   □ b. a coward at heart.
   □ c. openly violent.
   □ d. extremely superstitious.

7. From reading this story, we can infer that while Shadrack was in jail he
   □ a. wanted to stay.
   □ b. tried to find out who he was.
   □ c. remained drunk and disorderly.
   □ d. bothered the jailer.

8. The tone of voice most people eventually used when they spoke of Shadrack shows that the ultimate feeling about him was
   □ a. abusive.   □ c. angry.
   □ b. disrespectful. □ d. dispassionate.

9. Although he seldom acted sane, Shadrack still maintained his
   - ☐ a. independence.
   - ☐ b. disobedience.
   - ☐ c. ambition.
   - ☐ d. religion.

10. The sentence "A sleep deeper than the hospital drugs; deeper than the pits of plums, steadier than the condor's wing; more tranquil than the curve of eggs" shows the use of
    - ☐ a. comparison.
    - ☐ b. similies.
    - ☐ c. alliteration.
    - ☐ d. parables.

Comprehension Skills

1. recalling specific facts	6. making a judgment
2. retaining concepts	7. making an inference
3. organizing facts	8. recognizing tone
4. understanding the main idea	9. understanding characters
5. drawing a conclusion	10. appreciation of literary forms

Study Skills, Part One—Following is a passage with blanks where words have been omitted. Next to the passage are groups of five words, one group for each blank. Complete the passage by circling the correct word for each of the blanks.

Building Vocabulary

There is a vital connection between language and learning ability and between good grades and the ability to communicate your thoughts clearly and accurately.

An academic curriculum incorporates many subjects, each of which is characterized by its own vocabulary of __(1)__ terms. These terms must be understood if the subject is to be mastered.

All teachers, when evaluating and grading students, __(2)__ those who can express their understanding of key concepts and fundamental facts clearly and concisely. Students display this kind of understanding through their use of __(3)__ terminology. Thus, familiarity with the vocabulary of a subject opens the avenues of communication between student and __(4)__ .

This is not to say that random flaunting of specialized terms will deceive instructors, but it stands to reason that as you acquire the vocabulary of a subject, you will also be accumulating fundamental knowledge in that field. This becomes the base on which new __(5)__ is acquired and assimilated during your regular study.

It is a fact that familiar material is more easily read and understood than __(6)__ material. This explains why we all tend to read articles in our field of interest with ease; we already have the necessary background of information. And this also explains why we sometimes find new subjects dull and uninteresting. Learning the basic vocabulary of a subject gives us a __(7)__ to build on and assures that our study of that field will be profitable.

(1) successive   borrowed
general   specialized   correlated

(2) reward   punish
appreciate   suspect   notice

(3) appropriate   random
useless   helpful   enthusiastic

(4) peers   friend
teacher   parent   employer

(5) words   friends
associations   learning   principles

(6) easy   new
old   difficult   technical

(7) motivation   orientation
introduction   foundation   dictation

Study Skills, Part Two—Read the study skills passage again, paying special attention to the lesson being taught. Then, without looking back at the passage, complete each sentence below by writing in the missing word or words. Check the Answer Key on page 107 for the answers to Study Skills, Part One, and Study Skills, Part Two.

1. The specialized vocabulary of a subject must be understood if the subject is to be _____ .

2. Knowledge of vocabulary enables a student to express his _____ of the key concepts of a subject.

3. Acquiring a specific vocabulary also adds to fundamental _____ in a particular field.

4. We read articles about familiar subjects with ease because we already have a _____ of information.

5. Unfamiliar materials often seem dull and _____ .

12 | The Heart of a Woman

by Maya Angelou

Vocabulary—The five words below are from the story you are about to read. Study the words and their meanings. Then complete the ten sentences that follow, using one of the five words to fill in the blank in each sentence. Mark your answer by writing the letter of the word on the line before the sentence. Check your answers in the Answer Key on page 107.

A. perversity: abnormality

B. predicament: an unfortunate situation

C. studiously: thoughtfully

D. taut: tightly drawn; tense, nervous

E. deprecating: disapproving

_____ 1. The _____ stares from everyone in the room made the speaker feel unwelcomed.

_____ 2. The first bit of criticism came from a small, _____ quiet man.

_____ 3. To ignore such good advice would have been only an act of _____ .

_____ 4. John Clarke was known for his _____ , tense disposition.

_____ 5. As Maya looked around the room, she realized her _____ and knew there was no escape.

_____ 6. Slowly, Maya lifted her eyes, only to be greeted by the _____ expressions of those around her.

_____ 7. With _____ calm silence, the captivated audience listened to the new speaker.

_____ 8. Maya's body was _____ as a bowstring as she tried to read her play.

_____ 9. The _____ of the situation Maya found herself in might have been humorous if she had not been so scared.

_____ 10. Maya was so nervous she was convinced that her _____ was life-threatening.

The Harlem Writers Guild was meeting at John's house, and my palms were sweating and my tongue was thick. The loosely formed organization, without dues or membership cards, had one strict rule: any invited guest could sit in for three meetings, but thereafter, the visitor had to read from his or her work in progress. My time had come.

Sarah Wright and Sylvester Leeks stood in a corner talking softly. John Clarke was staring at titles in the bookcase. Mary Delany and Millie Jordan were giving their coats to Grace and exchanging greetings. The other writers were already seated around the living room in a semicircle.

John Killens walked past me, touching my shoulder, took his seat and called the meeting to order.

"O.K., everybody. Let's start." Chairs scraped the floor and the sounds reverberated in my armpits. "As you know, our newest member, our California singer, is going to read from her new play. What's the title, Maya?"

"One Love. One Life." My usually deep voice leaked out high-pitched and weak.

A writer asked how many acts the play had. I answered again in the piping voice, "So far only one."

Everyone laughed; they thought I was making a joke.

"If everyone is ready, we can begin." John picked up his note pad. There was a loud rustling as the writers prepared to take notes.

I read the character and set description despite the sudden perversity of my body. The blood pounded in my ears but not enough to drown the skinny sound of my voice. My hands shook so that I had to lay the pages in my lap, but that was not a good solution due to the tricks my knees were playing. They lifted voluntarily, pulling my heels off the floor and then trembled like disturbed Jello. Before I launched into the play's action, I looked around at the writers expecting but hoping not to see their amusement at my predicament. Their faces were studiously blank. Within a year, I was to learn that each had a horror story about a first reading at the Harlem Writers Guild.

Time wrapped itself around every word, slowing me. I couldn't force myself to read faster. The pages seemed to be multiplying even as I was trying to reduce them. The play was dull, the characters, unreal, and the dialogue was taken entirely off the back of a Campbell's Soup can. I knew this was my first and last time at the Guild. Even if I hadn't the grace to withdraw voluntarily, I was certain the members had a method of separating the wheat from the chaff.

"The End." At last.

The members laid their notes down beside their chairs and a few got up to use the toilets. No one spoke. Even as I read I knew the drama was bad, but maybe someone would have lied a little.

To become a writer, Maya was learning, was hard enough. To be a member of the Harlem Writers Guild, she was about to learn, was to run a gauntlet of stinging criticism.

The room filled. Only the whispering of papers shifting told me that the jury was ready.

John Henrik Clarke, a taut little man from the South, cleared his throat. If he was to be the first critic, I knew I would receive the worst sentence. John Clarke was famous in the group for his keen intelligence and bitter wit. He had supposedly once told the FBI that they were wrong to think that he would sell out his home state of Georgia; he added that he would give it away, and if he found no takers he would even pay someone to take it.

"One Life. One Love?" His voice was a rasp of disbelief. "I found no life and very little love in the play from the opening of the act to its unfortunate end."

Using superhuman power, I kept my mouth closed and my eyes on my yellow pad.

He continued, his voice lifting. "In 1879, on a March evening, Alexander Graham Bell successfully completed his attempts to send the human voice through a little wire. The following morning some frustrated playwright, unwilling to build the necessary construction plot, began his play with a phone call."

A general deprecating murmur floated in the air.

"Aw, John" and "Don't be so mean" and "Ooo Johnnn, you ought to be ashamed." Their moans were facetious, mere accompaniment to their relish.

Grace invited everyone to drinks, and the crowd rose and started milling around, while I stayed in my chair.

Grace called to me. "Come on, Maya. Have a drink. You need it." I grinned and knew movement was out of the question.

Killens came over. "Good thing you stayed. You got some very important criticism." He, too, could slide to hell straddling a knotted greasy rope. "Don't just sit there. If they think you're too sensitive, you won't get such valuable criticism the next time you read."

The next time? He wasn't as bright as he looked. I would never see those snooty bastards as long as I stayed black and their asses pointed toward the ground. I put a nasty-sweet smile on my face and nodded.

"That's right, Maya Angelou, show them you can take anything they can dish out. Let me tell you something." He started to sit down beside me, but mercifully another writer called him away.

I measured the steps from my chair to the door. I could make it in ten strides.

"Maya, you've got a story to tell."

I looked up into John Clarke's solemn face.

"I think I can speak for the Harlem Writers Guild. We're glad to have you. John Killens came back from California talking about your talent. Well, in this group we remind each other that talent is not enough. You've got to work. Write each sentence over and over again, until it seems you've used every combination possible, then write it again. Publishers don't care much for white writers." He coughed or laughed. "You can imagine what they think about black ones. Come on. Let's get a drink."

Starting Time		*Finishing Time*	
Reading Time		*Reading Rate*	
Comprehension		*Vocabulary*	

Aside from being a well-known writer, Maya Angelou has worked as an actress, film director, lecturer, and musician. During the 1960s, she worked as an editor and reporter in Africa, becoming the first woman editor of an English-language magazine. She published several novels in the 1970s and wrote the screenplay and musical score for the film *Georgia, Georgia* in 1972. In 1975 she received the *Ladies Home Journal* "Woman of the Year Award" for Communications. Other honors include a Tony nomination for best supporting actress for her performance in the 1977 television series *Roots*, numerous honorary degrees, and a place in the Black Filmmakers Hall of Fame.

Maya Angelou is currently a member of Actor's Equity, the Director's Guild of America, and the advisory board of the Women's Prison Association.

Comprehension— Read the following questions and statements. For each one, put an *x* in the box before the option that contains the most complete or accurate answer. Check your answers in the Answer Key on page 107.

1. Maya's play was called
   - ☐ a. *Living and Loving.*
   - ☐ b. *Today Love. Tomorrow Despair.*
   - ☐ c. *Love not Today.*
   - ☐ d. *One Love. One Life.*

2. According to John Clarke, being a talented writer was not enough—to succeed an author must also show
   - ☐ a. humor.
   - ☐ b. perseverance.
   - ☐ c. sensitivity.
   - ☐ d. reverence.

3. The writer develops her ideas through
   - ☐ a. spatial description.
   - ☐ b. comparison.
   - ☐ c. order of importance.
   - ☐ d. time order.

4. The main point of this selection is to tell us how
   - ☐ a. Maya Angelou was accepted into the Harlem Writers Guild.
   - ☐ b. writers form and conduct critique sessions.
   - ☐ c. the Harlem Writers Guild selected new members.
   - ☐ d. Harlem writers went about getting their work published.

5. This selection hints that the head of the Harlem Writers Guild was
   - ☐ a. Maya Angelou.
   - ☐ b. John Henrik Clarke.
   - ☐ c. John Killens.
   - ☐ d. Sarah Wright.

6. In your judgment, which of the following statements is true?
   - ☐ a. Sylvester Leeks was a soft-spoken man.
   - ☐ b. Maya had good reasons to be nervous about reading her play.
   - ☐ c. John Killens was extremely self-confident.
   - ☐ d. Writers groups offer little support to their members.

7. From this passage, we can infer that John Clarke
   - ☐ a. once had an unhappy marriage.
   - ☐ b. was always in trouble with the law.
   - ☐ c. founded the Harlem Writers Guild.
   - ☐ d. disliked his home state of Georgia.

8. The selection ends on a note of
   - ☐ a. hope for Maya's writing.
   - ☐ b. humor mixed with joy.
   - ☐ c. defeat over Maya's performance.
   - ☐ d. revenge for Black writers.

9. John Clarke's personality may best be described as
   □ a. congenial.   □ c. humorous.
   □ b. abrasive.   □ d. sensitive.

10. This selection can be called a complete story because it
    □ a. teaches a moral lesson.
    □ b. relates personal experiences.
    □ c. has a beginning, a middle, and an end.
    □ d. follows all the rules of grammar.

Study Skills, Part One—Following is a passage with blanks where words have been omitted. Next to the passage are groups of five words, one group for each blank. Complete the passage by circling the correct word for each of the blanks.

Specialized Word Lists, I

The two prime sources of words for your specialized lists are your instructors and your textbooks.

Listen during class lectures for the words the speaker repeats and __(1)__ . These are likely candidates. Identifying key words will present no problem because experienced lecturers understand the limitations of their listeners. They know that major __(2)__ need the emphasis of repeated exposure. What would be in bold print in a textbook must be conveyed to students verbally. Be alert for unusual inflection and __(3)__ which may be given to certain words. These are considered important by the lecturer. Especially important terms are often written on the blackboard.

Listen to questions asked by the speaker. Oral __(4)__ is often used to draw greater attention to important points under discussion.

Another clue to identifying important words and ideas may be found in the length of time devoted to discussion of a single topic. Important points deserve __(5)__ time.

When you discover that a major term is being presented, try to record the __(6)__ definition or explanation given. Being a specialist, your instructor will use precise terminology when defining a concept. Be sure to capture new words exactly as they are used. Indicate with an asterisk or star in your notes that here is a word for your __(7)__ list.

(1) rotates   emphasizes
     discards   ignores   shouts

(2)   points   errors
     expectations   illustrations   performers

(3)   appreciation   pressure
     concealment   strain   stress

(4)   humor   quizzing
     statement   concept   explanation

(5)   more   special
     primary   less   standard

(6)   first   only
     supplementary   general   exact

(7)   shopping   general
     specialized   surplus   discard

Study Skills, Part Two—Read the study skills passage again, paying special attention to the lesson being taught. Then, without looking back at the passage, complete each sentence below by writing in the missing word or words. Check the Answer Key on page 107 for the answers to Study Skills, Part One, and Study Skills, Part Two.

1. Two prime sources for specialized vocabulary lists are your

   _____ and your textbooks.

2. Experienced instructors make it easy to _____ key words.

3. Important words are emphasized, _____ , and often written

   on the board.

4. The instructor also uses oral _____ to draw attention to

   important points.

5. Because he is a specialist, the instructor will use _____

   terminology when defining a concept.

13 | Anticipation

by Mabel Dove-Danquah

Vocabulary—The five words below are from the story you are about to read. Study the words and their meanings. Then complete the ten sentences that follow, using one of the five words to fill in the blank in each sentence. Mark your answer by writing the letter of the word on the line before the sentence. Check your answers in the Answer Key on page 107.

A. accession: attainment of power

B. gusto: relish, great enthusiasm

C. attire: apparel, clothing, costume

D. resplendent: dazzling, stunning

E. frenzy: a temporary madness

_____ 1. The beauty of the feminine form before him stirred the king's mind into a yearning _____ .

_____ 2. The rich, brightly colored brocades and shimmering gold created a _____ picture of unforgettable beauty.

_____ 3. The king's _____ to the throne had been a peaceful one.

_____ 4. To the uninformed visitor, the celebration resembled a massive _____ of eating, drinking, and dancing.

_____ 5. With much _____ the king began to anticipate the pleasures of his newest acquisition.

_____ 6. Most people were seen in native Gold Coast _____ .

_____ 7. The _____ costume of the king bespoke of his wealth and good fortune.

_____ 8. The line of _____ fell to the king's oldest son.

_____ 9. The old men began to recall their younger days with nostalgic _____ .

_____ 10. The young girl's gaudy _____ was completely out of character.

Nana Adaku II, Omanhene of Akwasin, was celebrating the twentieth anniversary of his accession to the stool of Akwasin. The capital, Nkwabi, was thronged with people from the outlying towns and villages.

It was in the height of the cocoa season, money was circulating freely and farmers were spending to their hearts' content. Friends who had not seen one another for a long time were renewing their friendship. They called with gifts of gin, champagne or whiskey, recalled old days with gusto and before departing imbibed most of the drinks they brought as gifts. No one cared, everyone was happy. Few could be seen in European attire; nearly all were in Gold Coast costume. The men had tokota sandals on their feet, and rich multi-colored velvet and gorgeous, hand-woven kente cloths nicely wrapped round their bodies. The women, with golden ear-rings dangling, with golden chains and bracelets, looked dignified in their colorful native attire.

The state drums were beating paeans of joy.

It was four o'clock in the afternoon and people were walking to the state park where the Odwira was to be staged. Enclosures of palm leaves decorated the grounds.

The Omanhene arrived in a palanquin under a brightly-patterned state umbrella, golden crown on his head, his kente studded with tiny golden beads, rows upon rows of golden necklaces piled high on his chest. He wore bracelets of gold from the wrists right up to the elbows. He held in his right hand a decorated elephant tail which he waved to his enthusiastic, cheering people. In front of him sat his "soul," a young boy of twelve, holding the sword of office.

After the Omanhene came the Adontehene, the next in importance. He was resplendent in rich green and red velvet cloth; his head band was studded with golden bars. Other chiefs came one after the other under their brightly-colored state umbrellas. The procession was long. The crowd raised cheers as each palanquin was lowered, and the drums went on beating resounding joys of jubilation. The Omanhene took his seat on the dais with his Elders. The District Commissioner, Captain Hobbs, was near him. Sasa, the jester, looked ludicrous in his motley pair of trousers and his cap of monkey skin. He made faces at the Omanhene, he leered, did acrobatic stunts; the Omanhene could not laugh; it was against custom for the great Chief to be moved to laughter in public.

The state park presented a scene of barbaric splendor. Chiefs and their retinue sat on native stools under state umbrellas of diverse colors. The golden linguist staves of office gleamed in the sunlight. The women, like tropical butterflies, looked charming in their multi-colored brocaded silk, kente and velvet, and the Oduku headdress, black and shiny, studded with long golden pins and slides. Young men paraded the grounds, their flowing cloths trailing behind them, their silken plaited headbands glittering in the sun.

The old Chief, bored with his forty wives, perked up when a new beauty danced into view. To have her he would pay any price; he would even pay twice.

The drums beat on. . . .

The women are going to perform the celebrated Adowa dance. The decorated calabashes make rhythm. The women run a few steps, move slowly sideways and sway their shoulders. One dancer looks particularly enchanting in her green, blue and red square kente, moving with the simple, charming grace of a wild woodland creature; the Chief is stirred, and throws a handful of loose cash into the crowd of dancers. She smiles as the coins fall on her and tinkle to the ground. There is a rush. She makes no sign but keeps on dancing.

The Omanhene turns to his trusted linguist:

"Who is that beautiful dancer?"

"I am sorry, I do not know her."

"I must have her as a wife."

Nana Adaku II was fifty-five and he had already forty wives, but a new beauty gave him the same new thrill as it did the man who is blessed—or cursed—with only one better half. Desire again burned fiercely in his veins; he was bored with his forty wives. He usually got so mixed up among them that lately he kept calling them by the wrong names. His new wife cried bitterly when he called her Oda, the name of an old, ugly wife.

"This dancer is totally different," thought the Chief; "she will be a joy to the palace." He turned round to the linguist:

"I will pay one hundred pounds for her."

"She might already be married, Nana."

"I shall pay the husband any moneys he demands."

The linguist knew his Omanhene: when he desired a woman he usually had his way.

"Get fifty pounds from the chief treasurer, find the relatives, give them the money and when she is in my palace tonight I shall give her the balance of the fifty pounds. Give the linguist staff to Kojo and begin your investigations now."

Nana Adaku II was a fast worker. He was like men all over the world when they are stirred by feminine charm: a shapely leg, the flash of an eye, the quiver of a nostril, the timbre of a voice, and the male species becomes frenzy personified. Many men go through this sort of mania until they reach their dotage. The cynics among them treat women with a little flattery, bland tolerance, and take fine care not to become seriously entangled for life. Women, on the other hand, use quite a lot of common sense: They are not particularly thrilled by the physical charms of a man; if his pockets are heavy and his income sure, he is a good matrimonial risk. But there is evolving a new type of hardheaded modern woman who insists on the perfect lover as well as an income and other necessaries, or stays forever from the unbliss of marriage.

By 6 P.M. Nana Adaku II was getting bored with the whole assembly and very glad to get into his palanquin.

The state umbrellas danced, the chiefs sat again in their palanquins, the crowd cheered wildly, the drums beat. Soon the shadows of evening fell and the enclosures of palm leaves in the state park stood empty and deserted.

The Omanhene had taken his bath after dusk and changed into a gold and green brocaded cloth. Two male servants stood on either side and fanned him with large ostrich feathers as he reclined on a velvet-cushioned settee in his private sitting room. An envelope containing fifty golden sovereigns was near him. He knew his linguist as a man of tact and diplomacy and he was sure that night would bring a wife to help him celebrate the anniversary of his accession to the Akwasin Stool.

He must have dozed. When he woke up the young woman was kneeling by his feet. He raised her onto the settee.

"Were you pleased to come?"

"I was pleased to do Nana's bidding."

"Good girl. What is your name?"

"Effua, my lord and master."

"It is a beautiful name, and you are a beautiful woman too. Here are fifty gold sovereigns, the balance of the marriage dowry. We will marry privately tonight and do the necessary custom afterward." Nana Adaku II is not the first man to use this technique. Civilized, semi-civilized and primitive men all over the world have said the very same thing in nearly the same words.

"I shall give the money to my mother," said the sensible girl. "She is in the corridor. May I?" The Chief nodded assent.

Effua returned.

"Nana, my mother and other relatives want to thank you for the hundred pounds."

"There is no need, my beauty," and he played with the ivory beads lying so snugly on her bosom.

"They think you must have noticed some extraordinary charm in me for you to have spent so much money," she smiled shyly at the Omanhene.

"But, my dear, you are charming. Haven't they eyes?"

"But, Nana, I cannot understand it myself."

"You cannot, you modest woman. Look at yourself in that long mirror over there."

The girl smiled mischievously, went to the mirror, looked at herself. She came back and sat on the settee and leaned her head on his bosom.

"You are a lovely girl, Effua." He caressed her shiny black hair, so artistically plaited.

"But, my master, I have always been like this, haven't I?"

"I suppose so, beautiful, but I only saw you today."

"You only saw me today?"

"Today."

"Have you forgotten?"

"Forgotten what, my love?"

"You paid fifty pounds . . . and married me two years ago."

Starting Time		Finishing Time	
Reading Time		Reading Rate	
Comprehension		Vocabulary	

Comprehension— Read the following questions and statements. For each one, put an x in the box before the option that contains the most complete or accurate answer. Check your answers in the Answer Key on page 107.

1. Nana Adaku II had been on the throne for
   □ a. five years.
   □ b. ten years.
   □ c. fifteen years.
   □ d. twenty years.

2. At his stage in life, the Omanhene of Akwasin felt
   □ a. jaded.
   □ b. bewildered.
   □ c. content.
   □ d. proud.

3. The facts in this story are presented
   □ a. over a period of a week.
   □ b. within a three-hour time span.
   □ c. throughout a lifetime.
   □ d. as future happenings.

4. Disregarding the surprise ending, which saying below best suits the selection?
   □ a. There is no fool like an old fool.
   □ b. All that glitters is not gold.
   □ c. Charity begins at home.
   □ d. The grass is always greener on the other side of the fence.

5. We can guess that the story takes place in
   □ a. Africa.
   □ b. Asia.
   □ c. Europe.
   □ d. Australia.

6. The author suggests that women are somewhat
   □ a. sensitive.   □ c. calculating.
   □ b. emotional.   □ d. creative.

7. Effua's very first reaction to Omanhene was one of
   - ☐ a. disgust.
   - ☐ b. pity.
   - ☐ c. hysteria.
   - ☐ d. indifference.

8. The author's tone is
   - ☐ a. didactic.
   - ☐ b. light and somewhat humorous.
   - ☐ c. serious and rather scholarly.
   - ☐ d. nostalgic.

9. Nana Adaku II liked to be
   - ☐ a. independent.
   - ☐ b. humble.
   - ☐ c. indulged.
   - ☐ d. appreciated.

10. The selection is written in the form of
    - ☐ a. a court drama.
    - ☐ b. a narrative description.
    - ☐ c. an informal biography.
    - ☐ d. an ancient folktale.

Comprehension Skills

1. recalling specific facts	6. making a judgment
2. retaining concepts	7. making an inference
3. organizing facts	8. recognizing tone
4. understanding the main idea	9. understanding characters
5. drawing a conclusion	10. appreciation of literary forms

Study Skills, Part One—Following is a passage with blanks where words have been omitted. Next to the passage are groups of five words, one group for each blank. Complete the passage by circling the correct word for each of the blanks.

Specialized Word Lists, II

Another source of specialized terms is your textbook. Alert readers soon discover that a ___(1)___ frequently hinges on only five or six major concepts. Often there are key words associated with these concepts; these are the words to collect and learn.

Such words are often highlighted in bold print or ___(2)___ . If you need additional assurance, refer to questions or other types of summaries that frequently appear at the end of the chapter. These summaries will emphasize major points, the ones the writer wants you to understand and remember.

When you have ___(3)___ the important terms for the unit you are studying, write them down with accompanying definitions and explanations. As you read through the chapter, try to understand these new words and the concepts they represent as fully as you can. If you are not satisfied that your understanding is complete ___(4)___ your first reading, it may be necessary to reread parts of the chapter.

Frequently, these same words will be the ones that are emphasized in ___(5)___ . When this is the case, the instructor will often explain the new terms in words different from those in the text. Be alert to catch these variances because they ___(6)___ the meaning of an idea, often increasing its significance for you and making it easier to understand.

A ___(7)___ aspect of having studied and learned a term *before* class is that the speaker's remarks now make more sense to you. You will also find that your mind will wander less because of the greater interest and understanding that advanced knowledge fosters.

(1)	book	chapter
	paragraph sentence	phrase

(2)	commas	chapters
	headings periods	sentences

(3)	located	finished
	repelled created	lost

(4)	preceding	renewing
	during repeating	following

(5)	textbooks	class
	movies illustrations	studies

(6)	enrich	contradict
	specify define	change

(7)	miniature	repeated
	minus bonus	friendly

Study Skills, Part Two—Read the study skills passage again, paying special attention to the lesson being taught. Then, without looking back at the passage, complete each sentence below by writing in the missing word or words. Check the Answer Key on page 107 for the answers to Study Skills, Part One, and Study Skills, Part Two.

1. Key words associated with _____ points are the words to learn.

2. Questions and other types of _____ at the end of the chapter emphasize important points.

3. Write down important terms with accompanying _____ and explanations.

4. Instructors often add to the meaning of a word defined in the text and thereby _____ its significance.

5. Advance knowledge often produces greater _____ in and understanding of a subject.

14 | **Bloods**

by Wallace Terry

Vocabulary—The five words below are from the story you are about to read. Study the words and their meanings. Then complete the ten sentences that follow, using one of the five words to fill in the blank in each sentence. Mark your answer by writing the letter of the word on the line before the sentence. Check your answers in the Answer Key on page 108.

A. evade: to elude, to purposely avoid a situation

B. crucial: critical

C. saturate: to completely fill to capacity

D. portion: a piece of something

E. distinctly: unmistakably clear

_____ 1. In one battle, a large _____ of the platoon was killed.

_____ 2. I saved the rice, knowing that it would become a _____ part of my food supply.

_____ 3. Those who tried to _____ the draft found themselves facing a prison sentence.

_____ 4. The war was _____ etched upon the old soldier's mind.

_____ 5. The able general was determined to win the _____ battle.

_____ 6. The blood from so many dead or dying soldiers began to _____ the ground.

_____ 7. It was my job to stand guard and, if necessary, _____ the nearby jungle with gunfire.

_____ 8. You could not _____ the enemy when he was rushing right at you.

_____ 9. To say the least, my _____ of the chicken soup was small.

_____ 10. I can _____ remember the day Joe was killed.

I really didn't have an opinion of the war at first. I was praying that the war would bypass me. I chose not to evade the draft but to conform to it. I figured it was better to spend two years in the service than five years in prison. And I figured that for nineteen years I had enjoyed a whole lot of fruits of this society. I knew that you don't get anything free in this world.

Specialist 4 Strong recalls his service in the jungles of Vietnam and how he made his life-saving decision to get out.

I first arrived in Chu Lai in July 1969. After a week of orientation, I was assigned to the Americal Division, Alpha Company, 1st of the 96th. My company commander was a very good company commander, because he knew his profession and kept us out of a whole lot of crucial incidents. But the second lieutenant—the platoon leader—he was dumb, because he would volunteer us for all kinds of shit details to get brownie points. We would walk point two or three times a week for the whole company. He was literally the word "stupid," because he couldn't read a map. And he would say, "You don't tell me what to do, because they sent me to officers' training school." When we got one or two sniper fire, he would stop right there and call in artillery to saturate the whole area before you could take another step.

One time we had to check out an area. It was during the monsoon season. It rained 15 days and 15 nights continuously. We stayed wet 15 days. We started catching cramps and charley horses. And guys' feet got messed up. Well, they were trying to get supplies in to us. But it was raining so hard, the chopper couldn't get in. After five days, we ran out of supplies. We were so hungry and tired we avoided all contact. We knew where the North Vietnamese were, but we knew that if we got into it, they would probably have wiped a big portion of the company out. We were really dropped there to find the North Vietnamese, and here we was hiding from them. Running because we were hungry. We were so far up in the hills that the place was so thick you didn't have to pull guard at night. You'd have to take a machete to cut even 100 meters. It could take two hours, that's how thick the shit was. We starved for four days. That was the first time I was ever introduced to hunger.

Then we found some kind of path road down into a little village. And we came to a house that had chickens and stuff there. I think the people abandoned it when they saw us coming. I was the machine gunner, so I had to stay where I was and watch the open area while the guys searched the house. They were city guys who didn't know about utilizing the forest or what they were running into. So they started throwing the rice on the ground. They didn't have the experience that I had. When I was younger, I used to go out for miles of distance into the woods and run the snakes. I told my friend Joe to pick up the rice and get the chickens. So Joe got the stuff. I told them not to worry, so I skinned a chicken. I got a whole mess of heat tabs, and put the chicken in my canteen cup and boiled it for a long time. When I thought the chicken was half done, I put in the rice. And a little salt. It was about the only food we had until the bird came in two days after that. Those guys were totally ignorant. They kept calling rice gook food. That's why they threw it on the ground. I told Joe food is food.

It was a good thing that I didn't run in the house. Because I saw something about an eighth of a mile away. It looked like a little scarecrow out there in the rice paddy. It was sort of like a little sign. I looked at it real hard. I stretched my eye to make sure it wasn't nobody. Then I seen another little dark object, and it was moving. So I opened my fire immediately. I think the Viet Cong was trying to get around behind us so he could ambush us. I just happened to recognize him. I cut off maybe 50 rounds, and the CO hollered, "Hold up there, Charles. Don't just burn the gun up." The rest of the company told me I really got him, so that was the only person that I really was told I actually killed.

My feet was all scriggled up. My skin was raw and coming off. I still carry an infection on my feet right now that I have to visit the VA hospital on a regular basis to take treatment for.

Then I started to take drugs to stop the pain in my feet.

When one of our men was killed the next day, it didn't make a whole lot of difference, because I just felt good that it wasn't me. But it gave me a thrill like you take a drink of alcohol or smoke a cigarette to see a Viet Cong laying dead. It was giving me a good feeling. It stimulated my senses. I thought about it, and I really started to love seeing someone dead. And I started doing more drugs. Now I'm afraid that if someone catches me the wrong way, I would do them really bodily harm. It won't be no fight to prove who the best man is, or to prove manhood. Because of 'Nam, I cannot fight, because if I fight now, I'll fight for life. Someone is gonna die immediately.

But it hurt me bad when they got Joe. Joe was an all right guy from Georgia. I don't know his last name. He talked with that "ol' dude" accent. If you were to see him the first time, you would just say that's a redneck, ridge-runnin' cracker. But he was the nicest guy in the world. We used to pitch our tents together. I would give him food. He would share his water. And food and water was more valuable then than paper money. And when we had an opportunity to stand down, he would get sort of drunk and go around the brothers and say, "Hi there, brother man." The brothers would automatically take offense, but I always told them Joe was all right. His accent was just personal.

I remember one night I put my little transistor radio on my pack. We listened to music with the earphones, and he talked about his wife and kids back home on the farm in Georgia. He said he would be glad to see his wife. The next day he was walking point. I was walking the third man behind him when he hit a booby trap. I think it was a 104 round. It blew him up in the air about 8 feet. He came down, and about an inch of flesh was holding his leg to his body. He rested on his buttocks, and his arms were behind him. He was moaning and crying in agony and pain and stuff. What really got to his mind is when he rose himself up and saw his leg blown completely off except that inch. He said, "Oh, no, not my legs." I really distinctly remember the look on his face. Then he sort of went into semiconsciousness. He died on the way to the hospital. I had to walk up the trail to guard for medevac to pick him up. And I remember praying to the Lord to let me see some VC—anybody—jump out on that trail.

After six months, it was approaching Christmas, and we went back through the jungles to the rear area for a stand-down. That was when I made up in my mind that I wasn't going back to the field. The officers were dumb, but besides that, before I went to Vietnam, I had three dreams that showed me places in Vietnam. When we were in this one area, it was just like in the first dream. I felt like I had been there before, but I didn't place much value on it. But when I seen the second place, it dawned on me this was the place in the second dream. I said that in my dream, there's suppose to be a foxhole approximately 15 feet to the left and a little tin can sittin' on it. At the LZ I was in at the time, I walked straight to the place where the foxhole was suppose to be. And there it was. And the can, too. The third dream said that I was going to be crossing a rice paddy, and I was going to get shot in my chest with a sucking wound that I would never recover

from. And one of my buddies was holding me in his arms, saying I would be all right until the medevac came in. But it seemed like I never made it out of there. So I wrote my mother and told her that it was time to leave the field, or I would never make it out alive. The first and second dreams came true. It was a sign from the Heavenly Father for me to do something, or the third dream would come true. A Christian never walks into any danger, dumb and blind. Never.

Wallace Terry was born in New York City, educated at Brown, Chicago, and Harvard universities, and ordained in the Disciples of Christ ministry. He has produced documentary films on black Marines and served as a race relations consultant to General David C. Jones when Jones was commanding general of the United States Air Force in Europe. Terry has also been a radio and television commentator for various programs and has written for *USA TODAY.* In 1983 he was named to the Veterans Administration Advisory Committee on Readjustment Problems of Vietnam Veterans.

Starting Time   Finishing Time

Reading Time   Reading Rate

Comprehension   Vocabulary

Comprehension— Read the following questions and statements. For each one, put an *x* in the box before the option that contains the most complete or accurate answer. Check your answers in the Answer Key on page 108.

1. Joe came from
   - ☐ a. Georgia.
   - ☐ b. Virginia.
   - ☐ c. Mississippi.
   - ☐ d. South Carolina.

2. The writer leads us to believe that some officers were
   - ☐ a. amusing.
   - ☐ b. friendly.
   - ☐ c. wealthy.
   - ☐ d. incompetent.

3. The writer presents details according to
   - ☐ a. contrast.
   - ☐ b. spatial order.
   - ☐ c. cause and effect.
   - ☐ d. time order.

4. Choose the best title for this selection.
   - ☐ a. Facts About Vietnam
   - ☐ b. A Decision Based on Experience
   - ☐ c. A Soldier's Last Will
   - ☐ d. Life in a Monsoon Climate

5. How old was the author of this article when he entered the service?
   - ☐ a. 17
   - ☐ b. 18
   - ☐ c. 19
   - ☐ d. 20

6. We can make the judgment that the soldiers in this article
   - ☐ a. were not well equipped to face Vietnam's rainy season.
   - ☐ b. tried to overthrow their commanding officer.
   - ☐ c. were all graduates of a military academy.
   - ☐ d. had been properly trained in jungle survival.

7. We can infer that a machine gunner acts as a type of
   - ☐ a. medic.
   - ☐ b. scout.
   - ☐ c. clerk.
   - ☐ d. guard.

8. The last paragraph of the article leaves the reader with a feeling of
   - ☐ a. resignation.
   - ☐ b. enthusiasm.
   - ☐ c. pride.
   - ☐ d. urgency.

9. The company commander in this selection can best be described as
   - ☐ a. knowledgeable.
   - ☐ b. unwise.
   - ☐ c. agreeable.
   - ☐ d. jovial.

10. The one word sentence at the end of this passage is used as a point of
   - ☐ a. humor.
   - ☐ b. emphasis.
   - ☐ c. description.
   - ☐ d. information.

Comprehension Skills

1. recalling specific facts	6. making a judgment
2. retaining concepts	7. making an inference
3. organizing facts	8. recognizing tone
4. understanding the main idea	9. understanding characters
5. drawing a conclusion	10. appreciation of literary forms

Study Skills, Part One—Following is a passage with blanks where words have been omitted. Next to the passage are groups of five words, one group for each blank. Complete the passage by circling the correct word for each of the blanks.

Using Specialized Lists

You will naturally want your lists of specialized terms to be readily accessible and easy to use when you ___(1)___ them. There are different ways to accomplish this.

Some students list each word on its own 3 × 5 card along with the definition and an explanation. The cards can be filed alphabetically or by unit. Words recorded in this fashion are easily ___(2)___ , located, and reviewed.

Others prefer to use their notebooks. This arrangement allows new terms to be recorded close to the ___(3)___ accompanying the lecture or chapter where the new terms were first used. Words catalogued this way make reviewing easier since you are able to use your knowledge of the terms as an aid to recall important concepts from the lecture or text.

Each night new terms should be studied during the ___(4)___ and memorization segment of your study period. The words will then be fresh in your mind for class the following day.

Periodically, (___(5)___ midterm examinations, for example) all specialized terms should be reviewed and studied. It is prudent at this time to attempt to write the definition of each term from memory. It is important to recall the exact wording since precise definitions are more useful to you both in understanding the subject matter and for ___(6)___ your understanding to your instructor.

Studying word lists is not the only method of developing ___(7)___ .

Other ways include using contextual aids and studying word roots, prefixes, and suffixes.

(1) finish   see
         need   lose   find

(2) signaled   sorted
      diffused   collected   researched

(3) notes   illustrations
      bibliography   index   suggestions

(4) learning   preparation
      review   experimentation   presentation

(5) after   during
      following   before   replacing

(6) disguising   delivering
      defending   deducting   demonstrating

(7) phonics   vocabulary
      inference   scholarship   judgment

Study Skills, Part Two—Read the study skills passage again, paying special attention to the lesson being taught. Then, without looking back at the passage, complete each sentence below by writing in the missing word or words. Check the Answer Key on page 108 for the answers to Study Skills, Part One, and Study Skills, Part Two.

1. Index cards enable students to file new words _____ or by unit.

2. Words listed in the student's _____ can also be readily available.

3. New terms should be _____ each night.

4. Periodically, the student should attempt to write the definition of each term from _____ .

5. _____ definitions are more useful for understanding subject matter.

15 Brothers and Keepers

by John Edgar Wideman

Vocabulary—The five words below are from the story you are about to read. Study the words and their meanings. Then complete the ten sentences that follow, using one of the five words to fill in the blank in each sentence. Mark your answer by writing the letter of the word on the line before the sentence. Check your answers in the Answer Key on page 108.

A. nightstick: a policeman's stick or club

B. snipers: hidden gunmen

C. dig: to like or admire; to get the meaning of, understand

D. jive: phony; not desirable

E. torched: set fire to something

_____ 1. The old factory near my apartment had been _____ the night before.

_____ 2. Our group just could not _____ the ideas of Martin Luther King, Jr.

_____ 3. The students felt the principal's attitudes made school just one more _____ situation.

_____ 4. Everyone knew that the small corner fruit stand had been _____ as a means of protest.

_____ 5. Absentmindedly, the policeman twirled his _____ .

_____ 6. We had _____ positioned on every rooftop within view.

_____ 7. Not every black person could _____ our militant views.

_____ 8. That _____ school board sat there and agreed to every demand, even though not one person intended to keep the promises.

_____ 9. Somehow, when you fought the cops, you felt a sense of security because of the _____ on the roofs.

_____ 10. In desperation, the cornered youth picked up a discarded _____ and began swinging it violently.

That's the way it was. Seem like we was fighting cops every day. Funny thing was, it was just fighting. Wasn't no shooting or nothing like that. Somebody musta put word out from Downtown. You can whip the niggers' heads but don't be shooting none of em. Yeah. Cause the cops would get out there and fight but they never used no guns. Might bust your skull with a nightstick but they wasn't gon shoot you. So the word must have been out. Cause you know if it was left to the cops they would have blowed us all away. Somebody said don't shoot and we figured that out so it was stone rock 'n' roll and punch-up time.

Sometimes I think the cops dug it too. You know like it was exercise or something. Two or three carloads roll up and it's time to get it on. They was looking for trouble. You could tell. You didn't have to yell pig or nothing. Just be minding your business and here they come piling out the car ready to go ten rounds. I got tired of fighting cops. And getting whipped on. We had some guys go up on the rooves. Brothers was gon waste the motherfuckers from up there when they go riding down the street but shit, wasn't no sense bringing guns into it long as they wasn't shooting at us. Brothers didn't play in those days. We was organized. Cops jump somebody and in two minutes half of Homewood out there on them cops' ass. We was organized and had our own weapons and shit. Rooftops and them old boarded-up houses was perfect for snipers. Dudes had pistols and rifles and shotguns. You name it. Wouldna believed what the brothers be firing if it come to that but it didn't come to that. Woulda been stone war in the streets. But the shit didn't come down that way. Maybe it woulda been better if it did. Get it all out in the open. Get the killing done wit. But the shit didn't hit the fan that summer. Least not that way.

Lemme see. I woulda been in eleventh grade. One more year of Westinghouse left after the summer of '68. We was the ones started the strike. Right in the halls of good old Westinghouse High School. Like I said, we had this organization. There was lots of organizations and clubs and stuff like that back then but we had us a mean group. Like, if you was serious business you was wit us. Them other people was into a little bit of this and that, but we was in it all the way. We was gon change things or die trying. We was known as bad. Serious business, you know. If something was coming down they always wanted us wit them. See, if we was in it, it was some mean shit. Had to be. Cause we didn't play. What it was called was Together. Our group. We was so bad we was having a meeting once and one the brothers bust in. Hey youall. Did youall hear on the radio Martin Luther King got killed? One the older guys running the meeting look up and say, We don't care nothing bout that ass-kissing nigger, we got important business to take care of. See, we just knew we was into something. Together was where

For some young black men in 1968, everything—being in the streets, going to school, belonging to a militant group— was a political act.

it was at. Didn't nobody dig what King putting down. We wasn't about begging whitey for nothing and we sure wasn't taking no knots without giving a whole bunch back. After the dude come hollering and breaking up the meeting we figured we better go on out in the street anyway cause we didn't want no bullshit. You know. Niggers running wild and tearing up behind Martin Luther King getting wasted. We was into planning. Into organization. When the shit went down we was gon be ready. No point in just flying around like chickens with they heads cut off. I mean like it ain't news that whitey is offing niggers. So we go out the meeting to cool things down. No sense nobody getting killed on no humbug.

Soon as we got outside you could see the smoke rising off Homewood Avenue. Wasn't that many people out and Homewood burning already, so we didn't really know what to do. Walked down to Hamilton and checked it out around in there and went up past the A & P. Say to anybody we see, Cool it. Cool it, brother. Our time will come. It ain't today, brother. Cool it. But we ain't really got no plan. Didn't know what to do, so me and Henry torched the Fruit Market and went on home.

Yeah. I was a stone mad militant. Didn't know what I was saying half the time and wasn't sure what I wanted, but I was out there screaming and hollering and waving my arms around and didn't take no shit from nobody. Mommy and them got all upset cause I was in the middle of the school strike. I remember sitting down and arguing with them many a time. All they could talk about was me messing up in school. You know. Get them good grades and keep your mouth shut and mind your own business. Trying to tell me white folks ain't all bad. Asking me where would niggers be if it wasn't for good white folks. They be arguing that mess at me and they wasn't about to hear nothing I had to say. What it all come down to was be a good nigger and the white folks take care of you. Now I really couldn't believe they was saying that. Mommy and Geral got good sense. They ain't nobody's fools. How they talking that mess? Wasn't no point in arguing really, cause I was set in my ways and they sure was set in theirs. It was the white man's world and wasn't no way round it or over it or under it. Got to get down and dance to the tune the man be playing. You know I didn't want to hear nothing like that, so I kept on cutting classes and fucking up and doing my militant thing every chance I got.

I dug being a militant cause I was good. It was something I could do. Rap to people. Whip a righteous message on em. People knew my name. They'd listen. And I'd steady take care of business. This was when Rap Brown and Stokely and Bobby Seale and them on TV. I identified with those cats. Malcolm and Eldridge and George Jackson. I read their books. They was Gods. That's who I thought I was when I got up on the stage and rapped at the people. It seemed like things was changing. Like no way they gon turn niggers round this time.

You could feel it everywhere. In the streets. On the corner. Even in jive Westinghouse High people wasn't going for all that old, tired bullshit they be laying on you all the time. We got together a list of demands. Stuff about the lunchroom and a black history course. Stuff like that and getting rid of the principal. We wasn't playing. I mean he was a mean nasty old dude. Hated niggers. No question about that. He wouldn't listen to nobody. Didn't care what was going on. Everybody hated him. We told them people from the school board his ass had to go first thing or we wasn't coming back to school. It was a strike, see. Started in Westinghouse, but by the end of the week it was all over the city. Langley and Perry and Fifth Avenue and Schenley. Sent messengers to all the schools, and by the end of the week all the brothers and sisters on strike. Shut the schools down all cross the city, so they knew we meant business. Knew they had to listen. The whole Board of Education came to Westinghouse and we told the principal to his face he had to go. The nasty old motherfucker was sitting right there and we told the board, He has to go. The man hates us and we hate him and his ass got to go. Said it right to his face and you ought to seen him turning purple and flopping round in his chair. Yeah. We got on his case. And the thing was they gave us everything we asked for. Yes . . . Yes . . . Yes. Everything we had on the list. Sat there just as nice and lied like dogs. Yes. We agree. Yes. You'll have a new principal. I couldn't believe it. Didn't even have to curse them out or nothing. Didn't even raise my voice cause it was yes to this and yes to that before the words out my mouth good.

John Edgar Wideman was born and raised in the tough Homewood area of Pittsburgh, Pennsylvania, and began writing as a student at the University of Pennsylvania. As the second black Rhodes Scholar ever, he took a degree in English from Oxford University.

Wideman's books include the nonfiction *Brothers and Keepers* and a novel, *Sent for You Yesterday*, which is a PEN/Faulkner Award winner. He also contributes articles, short stories, book reviews, and poetry to various periodicals. Wideman is currently a professor of Afro-American studies at the University of Wyoming in Laramie.

Starting Time		*Finishing Time*	
Reading Time		*Reading Rate*	
Comprehension		*Vocabulary*	

Comprehension— Read the following questions and statements. For each one, put an *x* in the box before the option that contains the most complete or accurate answer. Check your answers in the Answer Key on page 108.

1. The name of the author's militant group is
   - ☐ a. Power.
   - ☐ b. Westinghouse.
   - ☐ c. Together.
   - ☐ d. Homewood.

2. The reader is led to believe that
   - ☐ a. Martin Luther King's views were too peaceful for the author.
   - ☐ b. the author is a hardened street criminal.
   - ☐ c. violence and disruption are part of all black people's lives.
   - ☐ d. education is worthless in the ghetto.

3. The facts in this story are presented mainly in
   - ☐ a. descending order.
   - ☐ b. spatial order.
   - ☐ c. a simple list.
   - ☐ d. time order.

4. Which of the following best states the governing principle of the author and his organization?
   - ☐ a. equality through militant action
   - ☐ b. Peace is the goal of all unrest.
   - ☐ c. Keep calm and success will triumph.
   - ☐ d. here today and gone tomorrow

5. When the writer lived through the events of the story, he was a
   - ☐ a. small child.
   - ☐ b. teenager.
   - ☐ c. young adult.
   - ☐ d. middle-aged adult.

6. We can judge from this passage that the author's mother
   - ☐ a. hates white people.
   - ☐ b. is a militant leader.
   - ☐ c. values education.
   - ☐ d. despises her son.

7. When members of the Board of Education came to Westinghouse High School, their attitude was one of
   - ☐ a. resistance.
   - ☐ b. resolution.
   - ☐ c. non-compliance.
   - ☐ d. opposition.

8. The overall tone of this article is
   - ☐ a. peaceful.
   - ☐ b. nonaggressive.
   - ☐ c. grateful.
   - ☐ d. militant.

9. How did the author feel when he spoke on stage?
   - ☐ a. important
   - ☐ b. frightened
   - ☐ c. unsure
   - ☐ d. humble

10. This selection is a type of
   - ☐ a. science fiction.
   - ☐ b. biography.
   - ☐ c. autobiography.
   - ☐ d. fantasy.

Study Skills, Part One—Following is a passage with blanks where words have been omitted. Next to the passage are groups of five words, one group for each blank. Complete the passage by circling the correct word for each of the blanks.

Other Word Study, I

1. Contextual Aids. By seeing a word in context, we come to know it better and better with every exposure. At first, the word becomes part of our ___(1)___ vocabulary. This means that we have seen it often enough to recognize it and remember its meaning. Many words remain just in our reading vocabulary. Other new words are repeated in print often enough for us to come to know them well; these words are then assimilated into our ___(2)___ vocabulary. In effect, we are confident enough to use the word in our writing. When a word finally becomes totally ___(3)___ , it may join our speaking vocabulary.

When read in context, words often have different shades of meaning that are imperceptible when initially read from a ___(4)___ . A simple word like *root*, for example, has at least 22 different meanings. The word *perception* has very different meanings in law and in psychology. You can't even know how to pronounce *precedent*, let alone know its meaning, without seeing how it is being used. And the only way to avoid the ___(5)___ between words like *precept* and *percept* is to learn them in context.

Further, relating a word to the way it is used increases our understanding not only of the word, but also of the idea the word represents. Consequently, words learned though context are more ___(6)___ than those learned from lists.

2. Affixes and Roots. Still another kind of ___(7)___ study centers around prefixes, suffixes, and roots. Because both prefixes and suffixes are added to words, they are collectively called affixes.

(1)   writing   speaking   reading   specialized   general

(2)   writing   listening   future   spelling   daily

(3)   obscure   familiar   forgotten   appreciated   analyzed

(4)   play   book   list   sentence   magazine

(5)   relationship   association   friction   stress   confusion

(6)   permanent   flexible   temporary   definite   enjoyable

(7)   unit   sentence   word   paragraph   chapter

Study Skills, Part Two—Read the study skills passage again, paying special attention to the lesson being taught. Then, without looking back at the passage, complete each sentence below by writing in the missing word or words. Check the Answer Key on page 108 for the answers to Study Skills, Part One, and Study Skills, Part Two.

1. Every time we see a word in context we get to know it _____ .

2. When we know a word completely it becomes part of our _____ vocabulary.

3. Some _____ of meaning are imperceptible when they are not read in context.

4. When we read a word in context we relate the word to the way it is _____ .

5. Prefixes and suffixes are both _____ to words.

16 | Let the Trumpet Sound

by Stephen B. Oates

Vocabulary—The five words below are from the story you are about to read. Study the words and their meanings. Then complete the ten sentences that follow, using one of the five words to fill in the blank in each sentence. Mark your answer by writing the letter of the word on the line before the sentence. Check your answers in the Answer Key on page 108.

A. precocious: showing mature qualities at an early age

B. rollicking: lively

C. recounted: narrated

D. counseled: advised

E. rancid: foul-smelling

_____ 1. Everyone at the party had a _____ good time.

_____ 2. When the _____ young boy began to speak, all those present listened in awe.

_____ 3. The congregation picked up the_____ beat of the song and began clapping in time.

_____ 4. The door to the men's room was left ajar, allowing the _____ fumes to permeate the large auditorium.

_____ 5. M. L. sat and listened while his mother _____ him about pride and self-esteem.

_____ 6. The old man _____ his life for the young child.

_____ 7. The parents knew that the _____ ways of their son would steer him toward greatness.

_____ 8. The class sat in stunned silence as the lecturer _____ the history of black people in American society.

_____ 9. The _____ meat was the only bit of food the prisoner was allowed.

_____ 10. For two hours the newcomers were _____ by the veterans in the room.

The adults remarked about how intelligent he was, how he could see and feel things beyond the understanding of most children, how he could drive you to distraction with all his questions. When his family rode through Atlanta, he observed all the Negroes standing in breadlines and asked his parents about them. It was the middle of the Depression, and 65 percent of Atlanta's black population was on public relief. M. L. was deeply affected by the sight of those tattered folk, worried lest their children not have enough to eat.

Yes, the adults said, he was a brilliant child, a gifted child, who could talk like he was grown sometimes. My, how that boy loved language. "You just wait and see," he once told his parents. "When I grow up I'm going to get me some big words." "Even before he could read," his Daddy boasted, "he kept books around him, he just liked the idea of having them." And his memory was phenomenal. By age five, he could recite whole Biblical passages and sing entire hymns from memory. His parents and grandmother all praised him for his precocious ways, making him flush with self-esteem. In fact, he was so bright that his parents slipped him into grade school a year early. Daddy recalled what happened next. "He was always a talkative chap, you know. So he shot his mouth off and told them he was only five while the other children were six, so they booted him right out of that class."

At six, he began singing hymns at church groups and conventions, accompanied by Mother Dear on the piano. Now he belted out a rollicking gospel song, now groaned through a slow and sobbing hymn. He sang his favorite with "a blues fervor." It was "I Want to Be More and More Like Jesus." People often wept and "rocked with joy" when he performed for them. But he "didn't get puffed up," his Daddy related, and sat down quietly when he was finished. Frankly, all the fuss embarrassed him.

In his preschool years, M. L.'s closest playmate was a white boy whose father owned a store across the street from the King home. In September, 1935, the two chums entered school—separate schools, M. L. noticed. He attended Younge Street Elementary School with Christine, and there was not a single white child there. Then the parents of his friend announced that M. L. could no longer play with their son. But *why?* he sputtered. "Because we are white and you are colored."

Later, around the dinner table, he confided in his parents what had happened, and for the first time they told him about "the race problem." They recounted the history of slavery in America, told how it had ended with Abraham Lincoln and the Civil War, explained how whites eventually maintained their superiority by segregating Negroes and making them feel like slaves every day of their lives. But his mother counseled him, "You must never feel that you are less than anybody else. You must always feel that you are *somebody.*" He did feel that he was somebody. Everyone

Young M. L. had to learn more than he was taught at school. He had to learn the language and customs, the whys and wherefores, of a white society founded on prejudice.

told him how smart and sensitive he was, praised him for his extraordinary ways. Yes, he had an idea he was somebody. Still, this race trouble was disturbing. "As my parents discussed some of the tragedies that had resulted from this problem and some of the insults they themselves had confronted on account of it, I was greatly shocked, and from that moment on I was determined to hate every white person."

So it was that M. L. began his real education in Atlanta, Georgia. Oh, he studied arithmetic, grammar, and history at school, passing easily through the lower grades and transferring in the sixth grade to David T. Howard Colored Elementary School, where he was deferential to teachers, considerate of his peers, precocious and diligent as always. But as with other Negro children, his true education was to learn in countless painful ways what it meant to be black in white America. He found out that he—a preacher's boy—could not buy a Coke or a hamburger at the downtown stores. He could not even sit at the lunch counters there. He had to drink from a "colored" water fountain, relieve himself in a rancid "colored" restroom, and ride a rickety "colored" freight elevator. White drugstores and soda fountains, if they served him at all, made him stand at a side window for ice cream, which came to him in a paper cup. White people, of course, got to eat their ice cream out of dishes. If he rode a city bus, he had to sit in the back as though he were contaminated. If he wanted to see a new movie in a downtown theater, he had to enter through a side door and sit in the "colored section" in the back balcony. Of course, he could always go to the decrepit "colored" movie house, with its old films and faded and fluttering screen.

He learned, too, how white Atlantans loved their Confederate heritage, cherished the halcyon days when plantations and slavery flourished in the surrounding countryside. He witnessed all the fanfare that attended the world premiere of the motion picture *Gone With the Wind,* which opened in Atlanta on December 15, 1939, when he was ten. White Atlanta quivered with excitement when Clark Gable, Olivia de Havilland, Vivien Leigh and her husband Laurence Olivier, all came to town for the opening. There was a gala parade downtown, then a grand ball at the auditorium, festooned with Rebel flags. Here white Atlantans reveled in songs like "Suwanee River," "Carry Me Back to Old Virginny," and "My Old Kentucky Home," and danced waltzes like southerners of old. The next night more than 2,000 white Atlantans crowded into Lowe's Grand Theater to see what they fantasized was the world of their ancestors portrayed in living color, a world of cavalier gentlemen and happy darkies, of elegant ladies and breathless belles in crinoline, a world that was lost forever in the Civil War. With its coveted myths and racial stereotypes (a good "nigger" was a loyal and obsequious slave, a bad "nigger" was an uppity and impudent black who rode in the same buckboard with a Yankee carpetbagger), *Gone With the Wind* became one of the most popular motion pictures ever produced in America, playing to millions of whites all over the land.

This too M. L. learned: a good nigger was a black who minded his own business and accepted the way things were without dissent. And so his education went. He discovered that whites referred to Negroes as "boys" and "girls" regardless of age. He saw WHITES ONLY signs staring back at him almost everywhere: in the windows of barber shops and all the good restaurants and hotels, at the YMCA, the city parks, golf courses, and swimming pools, and in the waiting rooms of train and bus stations. He found that there were even white and black sections of Atlanta and that he resided in "nigger town."

Segregation caused a tension in the boy, a tension between his mother's injunction (remember, you are *somebody*) and a system that demeaned and insulted him every day, saying, "You are less than, you are not equal to." He struggled with that tension, struggled with the pain and rage he felt when a white woman in a downtown store slapped him and called him "a little nigger" . . . when he stood on the very spot in Atlanta where whites had lynched a Negro . . . when he witnessed nightriding Klansmen beat Negroes in the streets there . . . when he saw "with my own eyes" white cops brutalize Negro children. When his parents admonished him to love whites because it was his Christian duty, M. L. asked defiantly: "How can I love a race of people who hate me?"

Besides, he didn't think his Daddy really loved them either. His Daddy stood up to whites, the way Grandfather Williams used to do. Yes, Daddy was always "straightening out the white folks." He would not let white agents make collections at his house. He would not ride the city buses and suffer the humiliation of having to sit in a colored section. He would not let whites call him "boy." One day when M. L. was riding with his Daddy in the family car, a white patrolman pulled him over and snapped, "Boy, show me your license." Daddy shot back, "Do you see this child here?" He pointed at M. L. "That's a *boy* there. I'm a *man*. I'm Reverend King."

"When I stand up," King said, "I want everybody to know that a *man* is standing." "Nobody," he asserted, "can make a slave out of you if you don't think like a slave." "I don't care how long I have to live with the system, I am never going to accept it. I'll fight it until I die."

A professional biographer, Stephen B. Oates has researched and written biographies of Nat Turner, John Brown, Abraham Lincoln, William Faulkner, and Martin Luther King, Jr. In writing *Let the Trumpet Sound*, Oates utilized the Martin Luther King Collection at Boston University, collections at the Martin Luther King, Jr. Center for Nonviolent Social Change in Atlanta and other public and private sources.

Starting Time			Finishing Time	
Reading Time			Reading Rate	
Comprehension			Vocabulary	

Comprehension— Read the following questions and statements. For each one, put an *x* in the box before the option that contains the most complete or accurate answer. Check your answers in the Answer Key on page 108.

1. M. L. lived in
   □ a. New York City.
   □ b. Atlanta.
   □ c. Nashville.
   □ d. Little Rock.

2. The Kings were willing to forgive the whites because
   □ a. it was the only way to survive.
   □ b. the Kings wanted to be like the whites.
   □ c. the Kings were Christians.
   □ d. not all whites were prejudiced.

3. The details of this article are arranged
   □ a. spatially.
   □ b. in chronological order.
   □ c. as a simple list.
   □ d. in order of importance.

4. Which of the following might be the best title for this selection?
   □ a. The Dawn of Desire
   □ b. Freedom for All
   □ c. A Dream Come True
   □ d. A Rude Awakening

5. We can conclude that the Younge Street Elementary School was
   - ☐ a. not integrated.
   - ☐ b. old and rickety.
   - ☐ c. on the edge of town.
   - ☐ d. for white children only.

6. We can make the judgment that since M. L. was black,
   - ☐ a. he could not wear white clothes.
   - ☐ b. he was not allowed to enter movie theaters.
   - ☐ c. he was not expected to attend school.
   - ☐ d. he could not eat at the restaurant of his choice.

7. This article infers that
   - ☐ a. Reverend King was a militant leader.
   - ☐ b. M. L.'s view of society was formed at an early age.
   - ☐ c. Mrs. King held an unrealistic view of her station in life.
   - ☐ d. segregation was abolished during the 1930s.

8. In this selection, the writer uses tone
   - ☐ a. to highlight attitudes.
   - ☐ b. to express an opinion.
   - ☐ c. to amuse the reader.
   - ☐ d. to show fear.

9. Before he started school, M. L.'s view of the world had been
   - ☐ a. free of bitterness.
   - ☐ b. tainted by race hatred.
   - ☐ c. quite realistic.
   - ☐ d. humorous.

10. In the second paragraph, the writer reveals M. L.'s character through the use of
   - ☐ a. vivid description.
   - ☐ b. figurative language.
   - ☐ c. direct quotes.
   - ☐ d. shocking exclamations.

Comprehension Skills

1. recalling specific facts	6. making a judgment
2. retaining concepts	7. making an inference
3. organizing facts	8. recognizing tone
4. understanding the main idea	9. understanding characters
5. drawing a conclusion	10. appreciation of literary forms

Study Skills, Part One—Following is a passage with blanks where words have been omitted. Next to the passage are groups of five words, one group for each blank. Complete the passage by circling the correct word for each of the blanks.

Other Word Study, II

When a prefix is added to the beginning of a word, it causes a change in the ___(1)___ of that word. For example, the prefix *un-*, when added to a word like *happy*, gives the word a completely opposite meaning.

Suffixes are added to the ends of words. Although they do not affect the basic meaning of a word, suffixes frequently alter its part of speech. For example, a verb, *hate*, can become an ___(2)___ , *hateful*, when a suffix is added.

Word roots are often Latin and Greek ___(3)___ on which many of our English words are based. *Bio*, which means *life*, is a Greek root word. From it we get such English words as *biology, antibiotic,* etc.

Through the study of affixes and roots, you can get a better "feel" for the meaning of many new words. Understanding how a word has ___(4)___ its particular meaning makes it much more likely that the word will become a part of your vocabulary. Check each new word you encounter in a good dictionary. The origin of the root of the word is usually ___(5)___ .

As you become more familiar with words—their origins (etymology) and their formative parts—you will find that new and ___(6)___ words will be much less discouraging when you meet them.

Effective word use distinguishes the educated person. Throughout life, we are judged and ___(7)___ on the basis of our ability to communicate. Since you have the opportunity now to develop your vocabulary, start at once by using the means suggested in this selection and make words the servants of your mind.

(1) appearance   pronunciation
     meaning   spelling   value

(2) interjection   adverb
     adjective   exclamation   addition

(3) stems   branches
     customs   stories   beliefs

(4) lost   acquired
     changed   enriched   collected

(5) avoided   omitted
     mentioned   translated   explained

(6) encouraging   difficult
     irritating   appealing   effective

(7) adopted   rejected
     evaluated   evicted   sentenced

Study Skills, Part Two—Read the study skills passage again, paying special attention to the lesson being taught. Then, without looking back at the passage, complete each sentence below by writing in the missing word or words. Check the Answer Key on page 108 for the answers to Study Skills, Part One, and Study Skills, Part Two.

1. A prefix is added to the _____ of a word.

2. A suffix is added to the _____ of a word.

3. Word roots are often _____ on words of Greek or Latin origin.

4. To discover the origin of a word, one should consult a good

   _____ .

5. Effective word use distinguishes the _____ person.

A Man's Life

by Roger Wilkins

Vocabulary—The five words below are from the story you are about to read. Study the words and their meanings. Then complete the ten sentences that follow, using one of the five words to fill in the blank in each sentence. Mark your answer by writing the letter of the word on the line before the sentence. Check your answers in the Answer Key on page 108.

A. dispirited: discouraged and saddened

B. montage: a picture made up of many smaller pictures; a mixture

C. excruciatingly: painfully

D. tangible: capable of being perceived by touch

E. affected: imitated; assumed

_____ 1. The young actor convincingly _____ a British accent.

_____ 2. With a sad resolve, the _____ black man turned and walked away from his southern home.

_____ 3. To save his friend, the young boy swam through the _____ frigid water.

_____ 4. Suicide is the final cry of a severely _____ soul.

_____ 5. The faces before the speaker formed a _____ of fame and renown.

_____ 6. Hate and betrayal almost became a _____ presence in the courtroom.

_____ 7. Determination spurred the runner on to the finish line as his legs and chest began to ache _____ .

_____ 8. There was something nearly _____ in the air last night that foretold of impending doom.

_____ 9. The spring flowers formed a _____ of bright colors.

_____ 10. In contrast to his normal easygoing nature, the teacher _____ an air of explosive anger when he introduced the subject of militancy.

A Black at the Gridiron Dinner

At a Washington dinner, Roger Wilkins discovers a subtle and disturbing racism among the power elite.

When it was all over, a number of men had tears in their eyes, even more had lifted hearts and spirits, but a few were so dispirited that they went upstairs to get drunk. We had just heard the President and Vice-President of the United States in a unique piano duet—and to many old Gridiron Dinner veterans, it was a moving showstopper. To a few others, it was a depressing display of gross insensitivity and both conscious and unconscious racism—further proof that they and their hopes for their country are becoming more and more isolated from those places where America's heart and power seem to be moving.

The annual dinner of the Gridiron Club is the time when men can put on white ties and tails and forget the anxiety and loneliness that are central to the human condition and look at other men in white ties and tails and know that they have arrived or are still there.

The guests are generally grateful and gracious. But the event's importance is beyond the structures of graciousness because it shows the most powerful elements of the nation's daily press and all elements of the nation's government locked in a symbiotic embrace. The rich and the powerful tell many truths in jest about themselves and about their country. I don't feel very gracious about what they told me.

Some weeks ago, to my surprise and delight, a friend—a sensitive man of honor—with a little half-apology about the required costume, invited me to attend the dinner.

The first impression was stunning: almost every passing face was a familiar one. Some had names that were household words. Some merely made up a montage of the familiar faces and bearings of our times. There were Richard Helms and Walter Mondale and Henry Kissinger and George McGovern and Joel Broyhill and Tom Wicker and William Westmoreland and John Mitchell and Tom Clark (ironically placed, by some pixie no doubt, next to each other on the dais) and Robert Finch and Ralph Nader and, of course, the President of the United States.

One thing quickly became clear about those faces. Apart from Walter Washington—who, I suppose, as Mayor had to be invited—mine was the only face in a crowd of some five hundred that was not white. There were no Indians, there were no Asians, there were no Puerto Ricans, there were no Mexican-Americans. There were just the Mayor and me. Incredibly, I sensed that there were few in that room who thought that anything was missing.

There is something about an atmosphere like that that is hard to define but excruciatingly easy for a black man to feel. It is the heavy, almost tangible, clearly visible broad assumption that in places where it counts, America is a white country. I was an American citizen sitting in a banquet room in a hotel that I had visited many times. . . . This night in that room, less than three miles from my home in the nation's capital, a 60 percent black city, I felt out of place in America.

That is not to say that there were not kind men, good men, warm men, in and around and about the party, nor is it to say that anyone was personally rude to me. There were some old friends and some new acquaintances whom I was genuinely glad to see. Ed Muskie, who had given a very funny and exquisitely partisan speech (the Republicans have three problems: the war, inflation, and what to say on Lincoln's Birthday), was one of those. I was even warmly embraced by the Deputy Attorney General, Mr. Kleindienst, and had a long conversation with the associate director of the FBI, Mr. DeLoach.

But it was not the people so much who shaped the evening. It was the humor amidst that pervasive whiteness about what was going on in this country these days that gave the evening its form and substance. There were many jokes about the "Southern strategy." White people have funny senses of humor. Some of them found something to laugh about in the Southern strategy. Black people don't think it's funny at all. That strategy hits men where they live—in their hopes for themselves and their dreams for their children. We find it sinister and frightening. And let it not be said that the Gridiron Club and its guests are not discriminating about their humor. There was a real sensitivity about the inappropriateness of poking fun that night about an ailing former President but none about laughing about policies that crush the aspirations of millions of citizens of this nation. An instructive distinction, I thought. . . .

As the jokes about the Southern strategy continued, I thought about the one-room segregated schoolhouse where I began my education in Kansas City. That was my neighborhood school. When they closed it, I was bused—without an apparent second thought—as a five-year-old kindergartener, across town to the black elementary school. It was called Crispus Attucks.

And I thought of the day I took my daughter, when she was seven, along the Freedom Trail, in Boston, and of telling her about the black man named Crispus Attucks who was the first American to die in our revolution. And I remember telling her that white America would try very hard in thousands of conscious and unconscious ways both to make her feel that her people had had no part in building America's greatness and to make her feel inferior. And I remember the profoundly moving and grateful look in her eyes and the wordless hug she gave me when I told her, "Don't you believe them because they are lies." And I felt white America in that room in the Statler Hilton telling me all those things that night, and I told myself, "Don't you believe them because they are lies."

And when it came to the end, the President and the Vice-President of the United States, in an act which they had consciously worked up, put on a Mr. Bones routine about the Southern strategy with the biggest boffo coming as the Vice-President affected a deep Southern accent. And then they played their duets—the President playing his songs, the Vice-President playing "Dixie," the whole thing climaxed by "God Bless America" and "Auld Lang Syne." The crowd ate it up. They roared. As they roared I thought that after our black decade of imploring, suing, marching, lobbying, singing, rebelling, praying, and dying we had come to this: a Vice-Presidential Dixie with the President as his straight man. In the serious and frivolous places of power—at the end of that decade—America was still virtually lily-white. And most of the people in that room were reveling in it. What, I wondered, would it take for them to understand that men also come in colors other than white. Seeing and feeling their blindness, I shuddered at the answers that came most readily to mind.

As we stood voluntarily, some more slowly than others, when the two men began to play "God Bless America," I couldn't help remembering Judy Collins (who could not sing in Chicago) singing "Where Have All the Flowers Gone?"

So later, I joined Nick Kotz, author of "Let Them Eat Promises," and we drank down our dreams.

I don't believe that I have been blanketed in and suffocated by such racism and insensitivity since I was a sophomore in college, when I was the only black invited to a minstrel spoof put on at a white fraternity house.

But then, they were only fraternity brothers, weren't they?

Born in Kansas City, Missouri, Roger Wilkins received his law degree in 1956 from the University of Michigan. He practiced international law in New York City for several years before joining the Agency for International Development in Washington, D.C. From 1966 until 1969, Wilkins served as assistant attorney general with the United States Department of Justice. He then directed the Ford Foundation's domestic program until 1972.

A career change led Wilkins to the *Washington Post*, where his editorials dealing with the Watergate scandal helped earn the paper a Pulitzer Prize nomination. He held editorial posts with the *New York Times* before joining the staff of *Nation* in 1979.

Starting Time		Finishing Time	
Reading Time		Reading Rate	
Comprehension		Vocabulary	

Comprehension— Read the following questions and statements. For each one, put an *x* in the box before the option that contains the most complete or accurate answer. Check your answers in the Answer Key on page 108.

1. Which of the following famous figures attended the Gridiron Dinner?
   □ a. Lee Iacocca   □ c. Ralph Nader
   □ b. Geraldine Ferraro   □ d. Jimmy Stewart

2. This article leads us to believe that
   □ a. even the daily press is often racist.
   □ b. racism is an American dream.
   □ c. there will soon be a black president.
   □ d. government is unconsciously sensitive.

3. The facts in the article are presented in
   □ a. order of importance.   □ c. spatial order.
   □ b. time order.   □ d. descending order.

4. Which of the following statements best gives the main idea of this selection?
   □ a. The men in the room were full of open prejudice.
   □ b. Because the mayor had been invited all the insults were forgotten.
   □ c. America is still guilty of insensitivity and rascism, conscious and unconscious.
   □ d. It's encouraging to have a president and vice president who can laugh at themselves.

5. The author of this article evidently lives in
   □ a. Boston.
   □ b. Kansas City.
   □ c. New York City.
   □ d. Washington, D.C.

6. The writer of this article makes the judgment that protest over the years has been
   □ a. productive.
   □ b. futile.
   □ c. nonexistent.
   □ d. misplaced.

7. We can infer that may of the jokes that were told at the Gridiron Dinner were
   □ a. political.   □ c. sexual.
   □ b. religious.   □ d. racial.

8. The overall tone of this article is
   □ a. hopeful.
   □ b. bitter.
   □ c. loving.
   □ d. funny.

9. The actions of the author at the end of this passage show he is feeling
   - ☐ a. guilty.
   - ☐ b. depressed.
   - ☐ c. satisfied.
   - ☐ d. generous.

10. The setting for the article is
    - ☐ a. a large room.
    - ☐ b. a small courtyard.
    - ☐ c. a large civic center.
    - ☐ d. an outside arena.

Study Skills, Part One—Following is a passage with blanks where words have been omitted. Next to the passage are groups of five words, one group for each blank. Complete the passage by circling the correct word for each of the blanks.

Listening Effectively

A wise man once said that listening is the hardest thing in the world to do. Today, listening is a lost art for most people. Understanding listening faults is a prerequisite to overcoming them. Suggestions for improving listening help you to ____(1)____ poor habits and cultivate good ones.

Faulty listening leads to ____(2)____, and that can be the cause of many problems. There are those who feel, with good reason, that we might have universal peace if only people would really listen to one ____(3)____.

In industry, millions of dollars are lost annually as a result of poor listening. Consequently, it has become standard practice at most major companies to "write it down." Xerox, a leading corporation, has developed an employee listening improvement course that it now sells to other companies.

In school, many students fail to listen properly to instructions. After many exams we hear about those who lose credit because they did not follow ____(4)____.

LISTENING FAULTS

One of the causes of faulty listening is daydreaming. This is probably the most troublesome listening fault because it affects almost everyone. Frequently a speaker will mention some person or thing that triggers an ____(5)____ in our minds and we begin to daydream. When we return to reality and begin listening again, we discover that point three is now being presented and we have no ____(6)____ of points one and two.

Opportunities for daydreaming are abundant because people speak at a much slower rate than we can ____(7)____. Thus, when a speaker is talking at a rate of 125 words-a-minute, the listener's mind may wander off.

(1) compound   correct
improve   recognize   create

(2) misunderstanding   comprehension
communication   anxiety   boredom

(3) another   person
theory   group   alone

(4) distractions   ideas
directions   attitudes   assignments

(5) inspiration   order
activity   actuality   association

(6) relation   organization
recollection   admiration   recognition

(7) expect   imagine
listen   think   dream

Study Skills, Part Two—Read the study skills passage again, paying special attention to the lesson being taught. Then, without looking back at the passage, complete each sentence below by writing in the missing word or words. Check the Answer Key on page 108 for the answers to Study Skills, Part One, and Study Skills, Part Two.

1. Misunderstanding is caused by _____ listening.

2. In _____ , poor listening causes a loss of millions of dollars annually.

3. In school, students often lose _____ in exams as a result of poor listening.

4. Daydreaming is a fault that affects almost _____ .

5. A speaker will often mention something that will trigger an association in our minds and cause us to _____ .

Black Boy

by Richard Wright

Vocabulary—The five words below are from the story you are about to read. Study the words and their meanings. Then complete the ten sentences that follow, using one of the five words to fill in the blank in each sentence. Mark your answer by writing the letter of the word on the line before the sentence. Check your answers in the Answer Key on page 108.

A. idleness: inactivity; laziness

B. relented: yielded

C. installments: the parts of a serialized story

D. baffled: confused

E. alien: strange, unfamiliar

_____ 1. That anyone would willingly write a story was an _____ thought to most students in the class.

_____ 2. The boy sat quietly, and out of his _____ an idea was born.

_____ 3. Begrudgingly, the young boy _____ and told the truth.

_____ 4. The policeman was completely _____ by the odd turn of events.

_____ 5. The editor decided to print the lengthy story in three separate _____ .

_____ 6. Being the only black student in an all-white school made the young boy feel _____ .

_____ 7. The newspaper arranged to print weekly _____ of the Christmas story.

_____ 8. No one could understand why the teacher _____ and allowed the disruptive student back into the classroom.

_____ 9. The hot summer day inspired sheer _____ in everyone.

_____ 10. The young boy's success as a writer brought _____ looks from his fellow peers.

The eighth grade days flowed in their hungry path and I grew more conscious of myself; I sat in classes, bored, wondering, dreaming. One long dry afternoon I took out my composition book and told myself that I would write a story; it was sheer idleness that led me to it. What would the story be about? It resolved itself into a plot about a villain who wanted a widow's home and I called it *The Voodoo of Hell's Half-Acre*. It was crudely atmospheric, emotional, intuitively psychological, and stemmed from pure feeling. I finished it in three days and then wondered what to do with it.

The local Negro newspaper! That's it . . . I sailed into the office and shoved my ragged composition book under the nose of the man who called himself the editor.

"What is that?" he asked.

"A story," I said.

"A news story?"

"No, fiction."

"All right. I'll read it," he said.

He pushed my composition book back on his desk and looked at me curiously, sucking at his pipe.

"But I want you to read it *now*," I said.

He blinked. I had no idea how newspapers were run. I thought that one took a story to an editor and he sat down then and there and read it and said yes or no.

"I'll read this and let you know about it tomorrow," he said.

I was disappointed; I had taken time to write it and he seemed distant and uninterested.

"Give me the story," I said, reaching for it.

He turned from me, took up the book and read ten pages or more.

"Won't you come in tomorrow?" he asked. "I'll have it finished then."

I honestly relented.

"All right," I said. "I'll stop in tomorrow."

I left with the conviction that he would not read it. Now, where else could I take it after he had turned it down? The next afternoon, en route to my job, I stepped into the newspaper office.

"Where's my story?" I asked.

"It's in galleys," he said.

"What's that?" I asked; I did not know what galleys were.

"It's set up in type," he said. "We're publishing it."

"How much money will I get?" I asked, excited.

"We can't pay for manuscript," he said.

"But you sell your papers for money," I said with logic.

"Yes, but we're young in business," he explained.

"But you're asking me to *give* you my story, but you don't *give* your papers away," I said.

He laughed.

"Look, you're just starting. This story will put your name before our readers. Now, that's something," he said.

After the response to his first published story, it's a wonder Richard ever wrote again.

"But if the story is good enough to sell to your readers, then you ought to give me some of the money you get from it," I insisted.

He laughed again and I sensed that I was amusing him.

"I'm going to offer you something more valuable than money," he said. "I'll give you a chance to learn to write."

I was pleased, but I still thought he was taking advantage of me.

"When will you publish my story?"

"I'm dividing it into three installments," he said. "The first installment appears this week. But the main thing is this: Will you get news for me on a space rate basis?"

"I work mornings and evenings for three dollars a week," I said.

"Oh," he said. "Then you better keep that. But what are you doing this summer?"

"Nothing."

"Then come to see me before you take another job," he said. "And write some more stories."

A few days later my classmates came to me with baffled eyes, holding copies of the *Southern Register* in their hands.

"Did you really write that story?" they asked me.

"Yes."

"Why?"

"Because I wanted to."

"Where did you get it from?"

"I made it up."

"You didn't. You copied it out of a book."

"If I had, no one would publish it."

"But what are they publishing it for?"

"So people can read it."

"Who told you to do that?"

"Nobody."

"Then why did you do it?"

"Because I wanted to," I said again.

They were convinced that I had not told them the truth. We had never had any instruction in literary matters at school; the literature of the nation or the Negro had never been mentioned. My schoolmates could not understand why anyone would want to write a story; and, above all, they could not understand why I had called it *The Voodoo of Hell's Half-Acre*. The mood out of which a story was written was the most alien thing conceivable to them. They looked at me with new eyes, and a distance, a suspiciousness came between us. If I had thought anything in writing the story, I had thought that perhaps it would make me more acceptable to them, and now it was cutting me off from them more completely than ever.

At home the effects were no less disturbing. Granny came into my room early one morning and sat on the edge of my bed.

"Richard, what is this you're putting in the papers?" she asked.

"A story," I said.

"About what?"

"It's just a story, granny."

"But they tell me it's been in three times."

"It's the same story. It's in three parts."

"But what is it about?" she insisted.

I hedged, fearful of getting into a religious argument.

"It's just a story I made up," I said.

"Then it's a lie," she said.

"Oh, Christ," I said.

"You must get out of this house if you take the name of the Lord in vain," she said.

"Granny, please . . . I'm sorry," I pleaded. "But it's hard to tell you about the story. You see, granny, everybody knows that the story isn't true, but . . ."

"Then why write it?" she asked.

"Because people might want to read it."

"That's the Devil's work," she said and left.

My mother also was worried.

"Son, you ought to be more serious," she said. "You're growing up now and you won't be able to get jobs if you let people think that you're weak-minded. Suppose the superintendent of schools would ask you to teach here in Jackson, and he found out that you had been writing stories?"

I could not answer her.

"I'll be all right, mama," I said.

Uncle Tom, though surprised, was highly critical and contemptuous. The story had no point, he said. And whoever heard of a story by the title of *The Voodoo of Hell's Half-Acre?* Aunt Addie said that it was a sin for anyone to use the word "hell" and that what was wrong with me was that I had nobody to guide me. She blamed the whole thing upon my upbringing.

In the end I was so angry that I refused to talk about the story. From no quarter, with the exception of the Negro newspaper editor, had there come a single encouraging word. It was rumored that the principal wanted to know why I had used the word "hell." I felt that I had committed a crime. Had I been conscious of the full extent to which I was pushing against the current of my environment, I would have been frightened altogether out of my attempts at writing. But my reactions were limited to the attitude of the people about me, and I did not speculate or generalize.

Richard Wright was born near Natchez, Mississippi, in 1908. He moved to Chicago in 1927 and to New York City in 1937. He lived in Paris from 1946 until his death in 1960.

Wright became famous in the 1950s upon the publication of his first novel, *Native Son,* which initiated the genre of the black protest novel. *Native Son* was the first bestseller written by a black person and the first Book-of-the-Month Club selection by a black author.

Wright's other novels include *The Outsider* and *The Long Dream.* His autobiography, *Black Boy,* realistically depicts black life in the United States in the early twentieth century.

Starting Time		Finishing Time	
Reading Time		Reading Rate	
Comprehension		Vocabulary	

Comprehension— Read the following questions and statements. For each one, put an *x* in the box before the option that contains the most complete or accurate answer. Check your answers in the Answer Key on page 108.

1. The author's first name is
   - ☐ a. Tom.
   - ☐ b. Richard.
   - ☐ c. Jackson.
   - ☐ d. Jim.

2. How was the author made to feel after his story appeared in the newspaper?
   - ☐ a. proud
   - ☐ b. angry
   - ☐ c. jealous
   - ☐ d. guilty

3. The facts in the selection
   - ☐ a. show cause and effect.
   - ☐ b. reveal spatial development.
   - ☐ c. are arranged in a simple list.
   - ☐ d. are arranged in chronological order.

4. This selection could be titled
   - ☐ a. The Value of Intelligence.
   - ☐ b. Swimming against the Tide.
   - ☐ c. All Races of People.
   - ☐ d. Fame and Fortune.

5. The author of this article probably lives in the
   - ☐ a. North.
   - ☐ b. South.
   - ☐ c. East.
   - ☐ d. West.

6. Judging from this passage, it seems safe to say that many times other people shape our
   - ☐ a. children.
   - ☐ b. attitudes.
   - ☐ c. families.
   - ☐ d. wealth.

7. We can infer that Aunt Addie and Granny were
   - ☐ a. political.
   - ☐ b. sensitive.
   - ☐ c. generous.
   - ☐ d. religious.

8. The attitudes of the writer's family are reflected in their tones. Those tones convey
   - ☐ a. sympathy.
   - ☐ b. understanding.
   - ☐ c. gloom.
   - ☐ d. disapproval.

9. How does the author feel by the end of the episode of the short story?
   - ☐ a. determined
   - ☐ b. defeated
   - ☐ c. joyful
   - ☐ d. elated

10. The selection is developed through the use of
   - ☐ a. tall tales.
   - ☐ b. symbols.
   - ☐ c. conversations.
   - ☐ d. descriptions.

Comprehension Skills

1. recalling specific facts	6. making a judgment
2. retaining concepts	7. making an inference
3. organizing facts	8. recognizing tone
4. understanding the main idea	9. understanding characters
5. drawing a conclusion	10. appreciation of literary forms

Study Skills, Part One—Following is a passage with blanks where words have been omitted. Next to the passage are groups of five words, one group for each blank. Complete the passage by circling the correct word for each of the blanks.

Listening Faults

Closed-mindedness. We often refuse to listen to ideas and viewpoints that run __(1)__ to our preconceived notions about a subject. We say, in effect, "I know all I want to know, so there's no use listening."

Actually, this is an intellectual fault that leads to a listening problem. Closed-mindedness __(2)__ with learning by causing you to shut out facts you need to know whether you agree with them or not.

False Attention. This is a protective device that everyone resorts to from time to time. When we're not really interested in what a person has to say, we just __(3)__ to listen. We nod and make occasional meaningless comments to give the __(4)__ that we are paying attention, when actually our minds are elsewhere.

Intellectual Despair. Listening can be difficult at times. Often you must sit through lectures on subjects __(5)__ to understand.

Obviously, you'll never understand if you give up. The thing to do is to listen more carefully than ever; ask questions when practical and, most important, discuss the material with a classmate. __(6)__ the problem as soon as it appears. Catch up right away and you'll feel less inclined to adopt an attitude of futility.

Personality Listening. It is only natural for listeners to appraise and evaluate a speaker. Our impressions should not interfere with our listening, however. The content must be __(7)__ on its own merits.

(1)	conclusive		parallel
	contrary	adjacent	similar
(2)	disagrees		consents
	intervenes	interferes	unites
(3)	proceed		pretend
	refuse	offer	begin
(4)	intention		concept
	proof	impression	denial
(5)	hard		unpleasant
	easy	trivial	important
(6)	Forget		Welcome
	Ignore	Attack	Defend
(7)	judged		overcome
	enjoyed	rejected	accepted

Study Skills, Part Two—Read the study skills passage again, paying special attention to the lesson being taught. Then, without looking back at the passage, complete each sentence below by writing in the missing word or words. Check the Answer Key on page 108 for the answers to Study Skills, Part One, and Study Skills, Part Two.

1. _____ interferes with learning by causing you to shut out facts that you don't agree with.

2. False _____ is a protective device that we all use at one time or another.

3. If you do not understand something from a lecture, it is a good idea to _____ the material with a classmate.

4. The prompt solution of this problem prevents an attitude of _____ .

5. The speaker is less important than the _____ of the speech.

Aké

by Wole Soyinka

Vocabulary—The five words below are from the story you are about to read. Study the words and their meanings. Then complete the ten sentences that follow, using one of the five words to fill in the blank in each sentence. Mark your answer by writing the letter of the word on the line before the sentence. Check your answers in the Answer Key on page 108.

A. deception: the act of trickery

B. stricture: restriction

C. rapt: completely attentive, absorbed

D. outlandish: strange to the point of being odd

E. vied: competed

———— 1. For hours, the men sat in ———— silence before the black box.

———— 2. The older man's ———— was soon uncovered.

———— 3. The two men ———— for the lady's attention.

———— 4. The ———— faces of the children testified to the speaker's story-telling ability.

———— 5. The clown's ———— costume made the children giggle with delight.

———— 6. The owner, and no one else, controlled the lights; for a long time we lived by this ———— .

———— 7. I automatically rebelled against the ———— my father imposed upon my activities.

———— 8. The magician's ———— was flawless.

———— 9. The two families ———— for total control of the town.

———— 10. Before long, the child's ———— behavior began to annoy everyone.

Workmen came into the house. They knocked lines of thin nails with narrow clasps into walls. The lines turned with corners and doorways and joined up with outside wires which were strung across poles. The presence of these workmen reminded me of another invasion. At the end of those earlier activities we no longer needed the oil-lamps, kerosene lanterns and candles, at least not within the house. We pressed down a switch and the room was flooded with light. Essay's instructions were strict—only he, or Wild Christian could give the order for the pressing of those switches. I recalled that it took a while to connect the phenomenon of the glowing bulb with the switch, so thoroughly did Essay keep up the deception. He pretended it was magic, he easily directed our gaze at the glass bulb while he muttered his magic spell. Then he solemnly intoned:

'Let there be light.'

Afterwards he blew in the direction of the bulb and the light went out.

But finally, we caught him out. It was not too difficult to notice that he always stood at the same spot, that that spot was conveniently near a small white-and-black object which had sprouted on the wall after the workmen had gone. Still, the stricture continued. The magic light was expensive and must be wisely used.

Now the workmen were threading the walls again, we wondered what the new magic would produce. This time there was no bulb, no extra switches on the wall. Instead, a large wooden box was brought into the house and installed at the very top of the tallboy, displacing the old gramophone which now had to be content with one of the lower shelves on the same furniture. The face of the box appeared to be made of thick plaited silk.

But the functions continued to be the same. True, there was no need to put on a black disc, no need to crank a handle or change a needle, it only required that the knob be turned for sounds to come on. Unlike the gramophone however, the box could not be made to speak or sing at any time of the day. It began its monologue early in the morning, first playing 'God Save the King.' The box went silent some time in the afternoon, resumed late afternoon, then, around ten or eleven in the evening, sang 'God Save the King' once more and went to sleep.

At certain set hours, the box delivered THE NEWS. The News soon became an object of worship to Essay and a number of his friends. When the hour approached, something happened to this club. It did not matter what they were doing, they rushed to our house to hear the Oracle. It was enough to watch Essay's face to know that the skin would be peeled off the back of any child who spoke when he was listening to The News. When his friends were present, the parlour with its normal gloom resembled a shrine, rapt faces listened intently, hardly breathing. When The Voice fell silent all faces turned

When modern times came to the African town, along came electric lights, the radio, and Hitler.

instinctively to the priest himself. Essay reflected for a moment, made a brief or long comment and a babble of excited voices followed.

The gramophone fell into disuse. The voices of Denge, Ayinde Bakare, Ambrose Campbell; a voice which was so deep that I believed it could only have been produced by a special trick of His Master's Voice, but which father assured me belonged to a black man called Paul Robeson—they all were relegated to the cocoon of dust which gathered in the gramophone section. Christmas carols, the songs of Marian Anderson; oddities, such as a record in which a man did nothing but laugh throughout, and the one concession to a massed choir of European voices—the Hallelujah Chorus—all were permanently interned in the same cupboard. Now voices sang, unasked, from the new box. Once that old friend of Hallelujah Chorus burst through the webbed face of the box and we had to concede that it sounded richer and fuller than the old gramophone had ever succeeded in rendering it. Most curious of all the fare provided by the radio however were the wranglings of a family group which were relayed every morning, to the amusement of a crowd, whose laughter shook the box. We tried to imagine where this took place. Did this family go into the streets to carry on their interminable bickering or did the idle crowd simply hang around their home, peeping through the windows and cheering them on? We tried to imagine any of the Aké families we knew exposing themselves this way—the idea was unthinkable. It was some time, and only by listening intently before I began to wonder if this daily affair was that dissimilar from the short plays which we sometimes acted in school on prize-giving day. And I began also to respond to the outlandish idiom of their humour.

Hitler monopolized the box. He had his own special programme and somehow, far off as this war of his whim appeared to be, we were drawn more and more into the expanding arena of menace. Hitler came nearer home every day. Before long the greeting, Win-The-War replaced some of the boisterous exchanges which took place between Essay and his friends. The local barbers invented a new style which joined the repertory of Bentigo, Girls-Follow-Me, Oju-Aba, Missionary Cut and others. The women also added Win-de-woh to their hair-plaits, and those of them who presided over the local foodstalls used it as a standard response to complaints of a shortage in the quantity they served. Essay and his correspondents vied with one another to see how many times the same envelope could be used between them. Windows were blacked over, leaving just tiny spots to peep through, perhaps in order to obtain an early warning when Hitler came marching up the path. Household heads were dragged to court and fined for showing a naked light to the night. To reinforce the charged atmosphere of expectations, the first aeroplane flew over Abeokuta; it had a heavy drone which spoke of Armageddon and sent Christians fleeing into churches to pray and stay the wrath of God. Others simply locked their doors and windows and waited for the end of the world. Only those who had heard about these things, and flocks of children watched in fascination, ran about the fields and the streets, following the flying miracle as far as they could, shouting greetings, waving to it long after it had gone and returning home to await its next advent.

One morning The News reported that a ship had blown up in Lagos harbour taking some of its crew with it. The explosion had rocked the island, blown out windows and shaken off roofs. The lagoon was in flames and Lagosians lined the edges of the lagoon, marvelling at the strange omen—tall fires leaping frenziedly on the surface of water. Hitler was really coming close. No one however appeared to be very certain what to do when he finally appeared.

Wole Soyinka was born in Isata, Nigeria. He was educated at the University of Ibadan and received a degree from the University of Leeds in 1959. He has been a research fellow in drama, a senior lecturer in English, and professor of Drama at the University of Ife, Nigeria. In 1974, Soyinka left the world of academia to become an editor, playwright, novelist, and poet, as well as director of his own theatre groups.

Soyinka's many novels and plays concentrate on the conflict between the past and present, between tribal beliefs and modern expediency. He has received a Rockefeller Grant, the John Whiting Drama Prize, and the *New Statesman* Jock Campbell Award.

Starting Time		Finishing Time	
Reading Time		Reading Rate	
Comprehension		Vocabulary	

Comprehension— Read the following questions and statements. For each one, put an *x* in the box before the option that contains the most complete or accurate answer. Check your answers in the Answer Key on page 108.

1. The first and last song played every day on the new radio was
   □ a. "God Save the King."
   □ b. "Old Folks at Home."
   □ c. "The Hallelujah Chorus."
   □ d. "The Star-Spangled Banner."

2. What is the first modern convenience described in this article?
   □ a. the telephone
   □ b. electricity
   □ c. running water
   □ d. central heat

3. In organizing facts, the selection uses
   □ a. order of importance.
   □ b. descending order.
   □ c. cause and effect.
   □ d. time order.

4. Which of the titles below best suits this article?
   □ a. Open Jealousy
   □ b. Caring Too Much
   □ c. Silent Opposition
   □ d. Childhood Memories

5. We can conclude that the gramophone was a type of
   □ a. dictaphone.
   □ b. telephone.
   □ c. phonograph.
   □ d. polygraph.

6. Apparently, many of Essay's friends
   □ a. did not have a radio.
   □ b. went off to war.
   □ c. already had electricity.
   □ d. enjoyed watching television.

7. What would happen to children who interrupted Essay's news program?
   □ a. They would be sent to their room.
   □ b. They would be ignored.
   □ c. They would be whipped.
   □ d. They would go hungry.

8. The tone of this article is meant to convey
   □ a. confusion.
   □ b. caution.
   □ c. disgust.
   □ d. innocence.

9. Essay can be described as
   - ☐ a. domineering.
   - ☐ b. humorous.
   - ☐ c. sarcastic.
   - ☐ d. forgiving.

10. The writer of this selection seems most interested in
   - ☐ a. teaching a lesson.
   - ☐ b. presenting a wide range of facts and opinions.
   - ☐ c. outlining a plot.
   - ☐ d. conveying the sense of a time and place.

Comprehension Skills	
1. recalling specific facts	6. making a judgment
2. retaining concepts	7. making an inference
3. organizing facts	8. recognizing tone
4. understanding the main idea	9. understanding characters
5. drawing a conclusion	10. appreciation of literary forms

Study Skills, Part One—Following is a passage with blanks where words have been omitted. Next to the passage are groups of five words, one group for each blank. Complete the passage by circling the correct word for each of the blanks.

Good Listening, I

To help improve your listening habits, here are some positive steps you can take.

Prepare to Listen. Your attitude while attending class is important. If you feel that a particular class is a waste of time, you will obviously not be in the ___(1)___ to listen. It is difficult and almost impossible to get anything out of a lecture that you are not prepared for. To prepare, decide before class that the lecture period will be well spent; resolve to make it a ___(2)___ experience.

Another good way to prepare for a lecture is to keep ahead in your textbook and other required ___(3)___ . The more you know about a subject in advance, the more interested you will be in hearing what the instructor has to say about it. For prepared students, lectures become an ___(4)___ of ideas rather than a deluge of unfamiliar and seemingly unrelated facts.

Watch the Speaker. Don't take your eyes off of the speaker. When you look away, you invite ___(5)___ distractions that may compete for your attention. In class, you must listen with your eyes as well as with your ears.

Develop an awareness of the speaker's mannerisms. The gestures a speaker makes supplement his remarks. What a ___(6)___ does with punctuation, bold print, headlines, and italics, a speaker does with vocal inflection and body gestures. All speakers communicate ___(7)___ as well as orally. You must watch as you listen.

(1) position   place
   mood   location   condition

(2) depressing   frightening
   learning   helpful   recreational

(3) writing   reading
   singing   playing   running

(4) inspiration   exchange
   exclusion   expression   inspection

(5) oral   intellectual
   visual   physical   muscular

(6) actor   writer
   teacher   lawyer   student

(7) physically   spiritually
   mentally   socially   successfully

Study Skills, Part Two—Read the study skills passage again, paying special attention to the lesson being taught. Then, without looking back at the passage, complete each sentence below by writing in the missing word or words. Check the Answer Key on page 108 for the answers to Study Skills, Part One, and Study Skills, Part Two.

1. It is important to attend class with a good _____ .

2. You will be more interested in the subject of the lecture if you read about it in _____ .

3. For unprepared students, lectures can be a series of unfamiliar and _____ facts.

4. In class, you must listen with your _____ as well as with your ears.

5. The speaker's _____ supplement his remarks.

20 | The Harlem Rat

by John H. Jones

Vocabulary—The five words below are from the story you are about to read. Study the words and their meanings. Then complete the ten sentences that follow, using one of the five words to fill in the blank in each sentence. Mark your answer by writing the letter of the word on the line before the sentence. Check your answers in the Answer Key on page 108.

A. demanding: expecting a lot from a person

B. priority: precedence or preference

C. contemplating: thinking over carefully

D. glowered: stared with a threatening expression

E. suppressed: withheld

_____ 1. Fixing the heating system was not a high _____ of the landlord's.

_____ 2. The bored husband quickly _____ a yawn as he listened to his wife's list of complaints.

_____ 3. The tenants had reached a point where they were _____ some sort of action against the owner.

_____ 4. The baby's safety was the parents' highest _____ .

_____ 5. Over the years, Belle had proven to be very _____ .

_____ 6. Feeling frustrated, the wife sat and _____ at her husband's caustic remark.

_____ 7. Battle _____ his rising anger as he viewed the baby's blood-stained cheek.

_____ 8. For years, Battle and Belle had been _____ a move.

_____ 9. Battle _____ at the interviewer when the full reality of his situation became clear.

_____ 10. The _____ boss expected his workers to push themselves beyond all human limits.

As Battle Young strode home along Harlem's Lenox Avenue on an October evening in nineteen-forty-eight, he scarcely noticed the chilly wind or the passersby. He was too absorbed in his own anger.

He swung a lunch pail as he walked, a tall, lithe man in Army clothes, thick-soled boots, khaki trench coat and knitted cap. His brown face was strong-featured, and his brown eyes mirrored an eternal hurt, frustration, or anger. He was a veteran, discharged only a year, after three bitter ones in the Army.

Crossing One Hundred and Thirty-fifth Street and heading north, his mind searched for the easiest way to tell Belle that he had failed again to get an apartment in the new project going up on Fifth Avenue. He thought of how she wanted to get out of those dismal three rooms on One Hundred and Thirty-eighth Street, so that Jean, their two-month-old baby, would have "a decent place to grow up in."

Belle had cried, threatened, pleaded, scolded, ridiculed and tried just about everything else in what she thought was the best method to make him get out and find a place! "Other vets are finding places. Why can't you?" she would cry out whenever she heard of someone else getting an apartment.

"We're lucky to find this hole." He told her over and over again, explaining that he wanted to get another place the same as she did. But she had always been a demanding woman, he thought, remembering their school days in Richmond, Virginia. It had been her strong persuasion after his Army discharge that brought them to New York.

And then, when the city-owned project started up giving priority to veterans, Belle had been certain they would get in. But just this evening he'd stood in line for an hour, only to have the interviewer tell him, "You're making too much money, Mr. Young. Your income is about three dollars a week more than the law calls for." He had argued at first and finally stalked out in anger. And now he had to face another one of those terrible arguments with Belle. God! How he hated to fight with her!

He walked around an unconscious Sneaky Pete drinker sprawled on the sidewalk at One Hundred and Thirty-sixth Street, crossed and glanced toward the Harlem Hospital as an ambulance turned east. Well, he had to go home, he thought, walking on in silence, swinging his lunch pail and staring in through the windows of the bars, the greasy cafes and the candy stores.

At the corner of One Hundred and Thirty-eighth Street, he turned east, walked past two tenements and entered the third. On the stoop stood a half dozen teen-age boys and girls. Climbing two flights of creaky stairs, he stopped just at the top of the landing, put his key in the lock, and went in the door.

Belle could see the answer in his grimy face when he came in, but she asked the question anyway, asked it

Battle Young endured as best he could the crumbling ceilings, the cold water, even the roaches. Then came the final indignity.

hopefully, standing in the middle of the front room. "What did they say at the project, honey?" Her voice was soft but clear.

"Will you let me get outta these dirty clothes and catch a breath?" he snapped, and then turned away ashamed.

Belle took the pail from his hands, turned on her heel, and walked into the middle room. She was slender, and her skin was a delicate reddish tan. Her brown hair was held up neatly by a hair net. Brown eyes accented a snub nose and soft, full, unpainted lips. She wore a blue and red flowered house dress, and fuzzy blue slippers.

The small room was dimly lit. On an old-fashioned iron bed in the corner a tiny baby slept. This was Jean. Belle smiled anxiously as she peered at the baby. Satisfied that Jean was snug, she turned and inspected the small, round, black oil stove. The flame glowed through the vents in its side.

Belle shivered slightly, turned it up and silently cursed Kelly, the landlord, for not providing heat.

The ceilings were cracked and falling. The dirty gray plaster walls appeared to have once been buff. Ancient chandeliers had become loosened from the ceiling, and from time to time the crumbling electric wire insulation wore through and short-circuited, plunging the apartment into darkness.

Going down a short hall, Belle mashed a roach with her foot as it scurried across the floor heading for the kitchen. She put Battle's pail on the top of a wooden ice-box standing in a far corner and went to her stove. After half an hour, Battle came in wearing a tattered blue terry-cloth bathrobe. His stiff, black hair was cropped short, and he carried an evening paper. His face, now clean, wore an annoyed expression as he walked to a cracked, porcelain-topped table, pulled out a rickety chair, and sat down with a sigh. He glanced at the paper's headlines while Belle stirred a pot. Both looked up knowingly as the steam pipe clanged a staccato beat of an overhead tenant calling for heat.

"That damn water is cold again. The day I leave this filthy hole I'm gonna kick that lousy Kelly right in his can!" Battle stormed. "Ain't no need of sayin' anything to the super. Kelly won't give him no coal!"

"Again?" Belle commented with sarcasm. "It's always cold." Then, "What did they say, Honey?" She reached back on the table for Battle's plate.

"I'm making too much," Battle said, looking hopefully as Belle dished up a sizzling pork chop, steaming lima beans, and kale.

Belle exclaimed, pushing the plate of food before Battle. "Whadda they mean? You making too much. We can hardly buy bread and meat!"

Battle chewed a mouthful and swallowed. "Well, there's this law against a guy making more than thirty-six dollars getting in city housing projects."

"Did you show 'em your discharge papers and tell 'em about me and Jean?"

"Sure. But that don't mean nothing."

"Well, since we got to stay here why don't you try to make Kelly fix up a few things and paint?" Belle said as she sat down to her own plate of food.

Battle slammed down his fork, and looked Belle straight in the eyes. "Now don't you go nagging at me again. Haven't I cussed and threatened ever since we been here? And Brown in I-E was here long before us, and Kelly ain't done anything in his apartment yet!" He picked up the fork, speared a piece of meat and started chewing savagely.

But Belle wasn't satisfied. She pushed the food about her plate without interest, contemplating an appropriate reply. "Well, can't you think of anything else? Can't you go see somebody? Isn't there a law for his kind? Or do you want me to do it?"

Battle had heard this before. She always managed to imply doubts of his ability to do things the way a man should, hitting his weakest spot. "Look," he muttered through a mouthful of food, "do you want me to kill that bastard, and go to Sing Sing? 'Cause if I get into one more argument with him and he gets smart, I'm gonna hit him with the first thing I get my hands on!"

"Fighting won't get the place painted, but thinking out a few ways to make him do it might help a little!" she blazed. She hesitated a moment. "You never did go back to that tenants' meeting, like Mr. Brown asked you to. You and the rest of these folks ought to listen to Mr. Brown and get together. You can't do nothing by yourselves."

Battle glowered and broke off a bit of white bread. For a few minutes they both ate in silence. Noticing that Battle was almost finished with his food, Belle said, "There's no more meat or beans, just kale, but there's some rice pudding from yesterday, and—"

Battle sputtered suddenly, staring at the wall against which the table stood. A fat roach sluggishly made its way ceiling-wards, antennae waving.

"Well, knock him off for heavensake, and stop cussing!"

He reached down, pulled off a battered bedroom slipper and unceremoniously smashed the roach. They both looked disgustedly at the mess. Then, as Belle got up and turned toward the icebox, Battle tore a corner from the newspaper he had been reading and wiped the wall.

"I don't want any pudding now," he said just before she stooped to open the box.

"Well, why did you mash him, Mister nice-nasty?" She came back to the table, sat down, and pulled a pack of cigarettes from her dress pocket. Battle pushed his dishes back and continued to read.

Belle lit her cigarette and blew out the first puff. Her mind was busy trying to hit on the best way to mention their housing predicament again. Battle seemed to sense her thoughts, and he glanced at her from the corners of his eyes several times. "Honey—" she began. Battle stiffened physically and mentally, but he turned to the sports page as though he hadn't heard.

This always annoyed Belle. She reached over and snatched the paper from him. "I'm talking to you, man! If you don't get me and my baby outta this rat trap, I will!"

Battle suppressed a desire to shout back. Instead he just stared at her and then reached patiently for the paper. She jerked it out of his reach. "You can sit there like a knot on a log if you want to!" Belle blazed.

A whimper from the baby in the middle room went unheard by either of them. Battle raised himself half out of the chair, reached over and grabbed Belle's arm, twisting it, and pulled the paper loose. She began to scratch at him but stopped abruptly when an agonizing cry came from the baby. She released the paper, jumped up, and ran from the kitchen. The baby still shrieked while Battle shuffled the crumpled pages back into place.

"My God, Battle! Come here! It's a rat!"

As he dashed into the room, Belle held Jean in one arm, and inspected two rows of teeth marks on the baby's right cheek. Blood oozed from each mark.

"He bit her, Battle! Oh God! He bit her!" she wailed as her husband rushed in.

As Battle looked at the tiny blobs of blood, smothering anger arose.

"Better go and put some iodine on her," he told Belle.

He spun at a noise under the bed, and stomped viciously as a dirty gray rat the size of a kitten scampered across the room.

Gritting his teeth he looked into the bathroom where Belle painted Jean's bites.

"How late does Kelly stay in his office?" he asked so quietly it alarmed Belle.

"Eight. What you gonna do, Battle? Don't get into no trouble!"

"I ain't gonna start no fighting trouble, but I'm gonna make it hot for Kelly."

He went back in the room, opened a closet and pulled on his clothes. He glanced at a clock on a dresser that said seven-thirty P.M. He went back to the bathroom door.

"Then tomorrow I'm gonna go from door to door and tell everybody in the tenant council what happened."

Belle smiled as he kissed her lightly, and patted Jean's head.

He left and went to see the landlord.

Starting Time		Finishing Time	
Reading Time		Reading Rate	
Comprehension		Vocabulary	

Comprehension— Read the following questions and statements. For each one,
put an *x* in the box before the option that contains the most complete or
accurate answer. Check your answers in the Answer Key on page 108.

1. This story takes place in
   - ☐ a. 1942.
   - ☐ b. 1944.
   - ☐ c. 1946.
   - ☐ d. 1948.

2. Belle tried to prod her husband to action by
   - ☐ a. complaining to the landlord.
   - ☐ b. attacking his manhood.
   - ☐ c. joining the neighborhood council.
   - ☐ d. looking for a job.

3. Paragraphs seven and eight show
   - ☐ a. simple listing.
   - ☐ b. spatial development.
   - ☐ c. time order.
   - ☐ d. cause and effect.

4. The Harlem rat of the title is
   - ☐ a. Battle.
   - ☐ b. the interviewer.
   - ☐ c. Kelly.
   - ☐ d. the rodent.

5. After Jean was bitten by the rat, Battle
   - ☐ a. attacked Kelly.
   - ☐ b. became an activist.
   - ☐ c. hounded Belle.
   - ☐ d. packed his belongings.

6. Which of the following best reflects Belle's thinking?
   - ☐ a. Honest poverty hath no shame.
   - ☐ b. In union there is strength.
   - ☐ c. Problems are best resolved at home.
   - ☐ d. Tomorrow is another day.

7. Battle refused the rice pudding because
   - ☐ a. he had had enough to eat.
   - ☐ b. he did not like desserts.
   - ☐ c. he had lost his appetite.
   - ☐ d. it was stale.

8. The tone of the selection is one of
   - ☐ a. wishful thinking.
   - ☐ b. fearful anxiety.
   - ☐ c. depressing futility.
   - ☐ d. deliberate oppression.

9. Belle can be described as
   - ☐ a. a shrewish wife.
   - ☐ b. hopelessly dejected.
   - ☐ c. a careless housekeeper.
   - ☐ d. impatient and frustrated.

10. The author develops the relationship between Belle
    and Battle by using
    - ☐ a. description.
    - ☐ b. comparison.
    - ☐ c. dialogue.
    - ☐ d. facts.

Comprehension Skills

1. recalling specific facts	6. making a judgment
2. retaining concepts	7. making an inference
3. organizing facts	8. recognizing tone
4. understanding the main idea	9. understanding characters
5. drawing a conclusion	10. appreciation of literary forms

Study Skills, Part One—Following is a passage with blanks where words have
been omitted. Next to the passage are groups of five words, one group for
each blank. Complete the passage by circling the correct word for each of
the blanks.

Good Listening, II

Note Questions. Listen closely to questions asked in
class. When an instructor asks a question, he or she is
probably about to ___(1)___ something important and is
calling for your attention. This is an important signal
between a speaker and the listeners.

Speakers' questions are designed to help you listen and
learn. You should also notice questions asked by others
in the class. Student questions signal the instructor; they
indicate how the ___(2)___ is coming across. The instructor

(1)   discuss   dismiss
     approach   retract   omit

(2)   appearance   voice
     intention   enthusiasm   message

will elaborate and illustrate, repeat and paraphrase, to help the listeners understand the matter. Questions from both teacher and ___(3)___ are valuable; pay attention to them.

Listen Creatively. You should not think about other things while listening to a speaker; you must give your ___(4)___ attention to the speaker's words.

Ask Questions. If questions are not ___(5)___ during a class session, write your questions in your notebook and get the answers later.

Bring Questions to Class. Your attention is sharpened when you are listening for answers. If your instructor calls for class participation don't be afraid or shy about speaking up. Your attention is ___(6)___ most sharply when you are on the firing line; and if you are mistaken and are corrected in class, you won't be likely to forget the correct response at exam time.

Your success in school will depend largely on how well you listen in class. If applied, the suggestions offered here can substantially improve your ability in this ___(7)___ area.

(3) principal   employer
     student   friend   parent

(4) polite   partial
     superficial   entire   apparent

(5) probable   rejected
     announced   permitted   programmed

(6) attracted   denied
     focused   damaged   forgotten

(7) unimportant   vital
     attractive   neutral   controversial

Study Skills, Part Two—Read the study skills passage again, paying special attention to the lesson being taught. Then, without looking back at the passage, complete each sentence below by writing in the missing word or words. Check the Answer Key on page 108 for the answers to Study Skills, Part One, and Study Skills, Part Two.

1. Instructors use questions as a way to call for _____ .

2. The instructor's question is an important _____ between an instructor and the listeners.

3. When you listen, do not _____ about other things.

4. Your attention is sharpened when you are _____ for answers.

5. If you are mistaken and corrected in class, you will not _____ the correct response later.

Answer Key

Selection 1

Vocabulary

1. C	6. B
2. B	7. E
3. E	8. A
4. A	9. D
5. D	10. C

Comprehension

1. b	6. c
2. a	7. b
3. d	8. a
4. a	9. c
5. c	10. d

Study Skills, Part One

1. effectiveness 6. lure
2. introductory 7. devices
3. anecdote
4. concepts
5. significance

Study Skills, Part Two

1. paragraphs
2. printed page
3. announcement
4. previewing
5. words

Selection 2

Vocabulary

1. C	6. A
2. B	7. B
3. E	8. E
4. D	9. D
5. C	10. A

Comprehension

1. d	6. d
2. c	7. c
3. a	8. c
4. b	9. d
5. c	10. d

Study Skills, Part One

1. understand 6. flexible
2. similar 7. linger
3. composed
4. limitations
5. clarify

Study Skills, Part Two

1. idea
2. students
3. misunderstood
4. speed
5. new

Selection 3

Vocabulary

1. C	6. C
2. E	7. D
3. A	8. E
4. D	9. B
5. B	10. A

Comprehension

1. c	6. b
2. d	7. b
3. a	8. d
4. c	9. b
5. c	10. a

Study Skills, Part One

1. subject 6. Expect
2. facts 7. present
3. examined
4. introduce
5. logically

Study Skills, Part Two

1. facts
2. instructional
3. reasons
4. learning
5. study

Selection 4

Vocabulary

1. D	6. B
2. E	7. A
3. D	8. B
4. C	9. C
5. A	10. E

Comprehension

1. d	6. a
2. a	7. d
3. b	8. a
4. a	9. b
5. b	10. d

Study Skills, Part One

1. topic 6. comprehension
2. new 7. Consequently
3. essential
4. precisely
5. definition

Study Skills, Part Two

1. recognizable
2. italics
3. key
4. information
5. contribution

Selection 5

Vocabulary

1. B	6. D
2. D	7. E
3. B	8. C
4. A	9. A
5. C	10. E

Comprehension

1. a	6. b
2. a	7. d
3. d	8. d
4. a	9. c
5. b	10. c

Study Skills, Part One

1. implies 6. contribution
2. change 7. roles
3. preview
4. arouse
5. summing

Study Skills, Part Two

1. short
2. ending
3. introduction
4. concluding
5. functions

Selection 6

Vocabulary

1. C	6. A
2. A	7. B
3. D	8. E
4. C	9. D
5. E	10. B

Comprehension

1. c	6. a
2. d	7. c
3. c	8. d
4. d	9. b
5. c	10. d

Study Skills, Part One

1. recognizing 6. developed
2. obvious 7. techniques
3. final
4. important
5. summarize

Study Skills, Part Two

1. conclusion
2. facts
3. reviewing
4. speaker
5. moral

Selection 7

Vocabulary

1. E	6. A
2. C	7. B
3. E	8. D
4. B	9. D
5. C	10. A

Comprehension

1. c	6. d
2. a	7. a
3. a	8. d
4. b	9. b
5. d	10. a

Study Skills, Part One

1. described   6. progress
2. studying   7. habits
3. mastery
4. plods
5. aloud

Study Skills, Part Two

1. inflexible
2. 100 percent
3. specialized
4. taught
5. conditioned

Selection 8

Vocabulary

1. B	6. C
2. A	7. D
3. C	8. E
4. E	9. B
5. D	10. A

Comprehension

1. b	6. c
2. a	7. d
3. a	8. b
4. a	9. c
5. d	10. d

Study Skills, Part One

1. skilled   6. comprehended
2. analytical   7. appropriate
3. skimming
4. casual
5. nonproductive

Study Skills, Part Two

1. varies
2. slow
3. rapid
4. concepts
5. skimming

Selection 9

Vocabulary

1. E	6. E
2. D	7. C
3. C	8. D
4. A	9. B
5. B	10. A

Comprehension

1. a	6. c
2. c	7. d
3. d	8. b
4. b	9. c
5. c	10. d

Study Skills, Part One

1. specific   6. Paragraphs
2. employed   7. skipped
3. information
4. graphic
5. factual

Study Skills, Part Two

1. careless
2. study-type
3. title
4. definitions
5. reference

Selection 10

Vocabulary

1. B	6. E
2. C	7. B
3. D	8. E
4. A	9. A
5. C	10. D

Comprehension

1. a	6. c
2. b	7. c
3. d	8. c
4. b	9. b
5. a	10. d

Study Skills, Part One

1. impressive   6. difficult
2. value   7. fill
3. necessary
4. perform
5. trigger

Study Skills, Part Two

1. dynamic
2. Previewing
3. ideas
4. Rereading
5. easy

Selection 11

Vocabulary

1. E	6. A
2. A	7. D
3. D	8. B
4. C	9. C
5. E	10. B

Comprehension

1. b	6. a
2. d	7. b
3. a	8. d
4. b	9. a
5. c	10. a

Study Skills, Part One

1. specialized   6. new
2. reward   7. foundation
3. appropriate
4. teacher
5. learning

Study Skills, Part Two

1. mastered
2. understanding
3. knowledge
4. background
5. uninteresting

Selection 12

Vocabulary

1. E	6. E
2. C	7. C
3. A	8. D
4. D	9. A
5. B	10. B

Comprehension

1. d	6. b
2. b	7. d
3. d	8. a
4. a	9. b
5. c	10. c

Study Skills, Part One

1. emphasizes   6. exact
2. points   7. specialized
3. stress
4. quizzing
5. more

Study Skills, Part Two

1. instructors
2. identify
3. repeated
4. questions
5. precise

Selection 13

Vocabulary

1. E	6. C
2. D	7. D
3. A	8. A
4. E	9. B
5. B	10. C

Comprehension

1. d	6. c
2. a	7. d
3. b	8. b
4. d	9. c
5. a	10. b

Study Skills, Part One

1. chapter   6. enrich
2. headings   7. bonus
3. located
4. following
5. class

Study Skills, Part Two

1. major
2. summaries
3. definitions
4. increase
5. interest

Selection 14

Vocabulary
1. D   6. C
2. B   7. C
3. A   8. A
4. E   9. D
5. B   10. E

Comprehension
1. a   6. a
2. d   7. d
3. d   8. d
4. b   9. a
5. c   10. b

Study Skills, Part One
1. need   6. demonstrating
2. sorted   7. vocabulary
3. notes
4. review
5. before

Study Skills, Part Two
1. alphabetically
2. notebook
3. studied
4. memory
5. Precise

Selection 15

Vocabulary
1. E   6. B
2. C   7. C
3. D   8. D
4. E   9. B
5. A   10. A

Comprehension
1. c   6. c
2. a   7. b
3. d   8. d
4. a   9. a
5. b   10. c

Study Skills, Part One
1. reading   6. permanent
2. writing   7. word
3. familiar
4. list
5. confusion

Study Skills, Part Two
1. better
2. speaking
3. shades
4. used
5. added

Selection 16

Vocabulary
1. B   6. C
2. A   7. A
3. B   8. C
4. E   9. E
5. D   10. D

Comprehension
1. b   6. d
2. c   7. b
3. b   8. a
4. d   9. a
5. a   10. c

Study Skills, Part One
1. meaning   6. difficult
2. adjective   7. evaluated
3. stems
4. acquired
5. explained

Study Skills, Part Two
1. beginning
2. end
3. based
4. dictionary
5. educated

Selection 17

Vocabulary
1. E   6. D
2. A   7. C
3. C   8. D
4. A   9. B
5. B   10. E

Comprehension
1. c   6. b
2. a   7. d
3. b   8. b
4. c   9. b
5. d   10. a

Study Skills, Part One
1. correct   5. association
2. misunder-   6. recollection
    standing   7. think
3. another
4. directions

Study Skills, Part Two
1. faulty
2. industry
3. credit
4. everyone
5. daydream

Selection 18

Vocabulary
1. E   6. E
2. A   7. C
3. B   8. B
4. D   9. A
5. C   10. D

Comprehension
1. b   6. b
2. d   7. d
3. a   8. d
4. b   9. b
5. b   10. c

Study Skills, Part One
1. contrary   6. Attack
2. interferes   7. judged
3. pretend
4. impression
5. hard

Study Skills, Part Two
1. Closed-mindedness
2. attention
3. discuss
4. futility
5. content

Selection 19

Vocabulary
1. C   6. B
2. A   7. B
3. E   8. A
4. C   9. E
5. D   10. D

Comprehension
1. a   6. a
2. b   7. c
3. d   8. d
4. d   9. a
5. c   10. d

Study Skills, Part One
1. mood   6. writer
2. learning   7. physically
3. reading
4. exchange
5. visual

Study Skills, Part Two
1. attitude
2. advance
3. unrelated
4. eyes
5. gestures

Selection 20

Vocabulary
1. B   6. D
2. E   7. E
3. C   8. C
4. B   9. D
5. A   10. A

Comprehension
1. d   6. b
2. b   7. c
3. b   8. c
4. c   9. d
5. b   10. c

Study Skills, Part One
1. discuss   6. focused
2. message   7. vital
3. student
4. entire
5. permitted

Study Skills, Part Two
1. attention
2. signal
3. think
4. listening
5. forget

Bibliography

Angelou, Maya. *The Heart of a Woman.* New York: Random House, 1981.

———. *I Know Why the Caged Bird Sings.* New York: Random House, 1969.

Baldwin, James. *Go Tell It on the Mountain.* New York: The Dial Press, 1953.

———. "Sweet Lorraine." In *To Be Young, Gifted and Black,* New Jersey: Prentice-Hall, Inc., 1969.

Baraka, Amiri. *The Autobiography of LeRoi Jones/Amiri Baraka.* New York: Freundlich Books, 1984.

Blay, J. Benibengor. "Funeral of a Whale." In *An African Treasury.* Edited by Langston Hughes. New York: Crown Publishers, 1960.

Brown, Claude. *Manchild in the Promised Land.* New York: The Macmillan Company, 1965.

Brown, H. Rap. *Die, Nigger, Die.* New York: The Dial Press, 1969.

Brown, Sterling. *The Massachusetts Review.* Amherst: University of Massachusetts, 1966.

Cade, Toni, Bambara. "The Pill: Genocide or Liberation." In *Onyx.* New York: Onyx Publications, 1969.

Carmichael, Stokely, and Charles V. Hamilton. *Black Power.* New York: Random House, 1967.

Clarke, John Henrik. "The Origin and Growth of Afro-American Literature." In *Negro Digest.* Chicago: Johnson Publishing Company, Inc., 1967.

———. "The Boy Who Painted Christ Black." In *American Negro Short Stories.* Edited by John Henrik Clarke. New York: Hill & Wang, 1966.

Cosby, Bill. *Fatherhood.* New York: Doubleday & Company, Inc., 1986.

Davis, Angela. *Women, Race and Class.* New York: Random House, 1981.

Douglass, Frederick. *The Narrative of the Life of Frederick Douglass,* 1845.

———. *What to the Slaves Is the Fourth of July?* 1852.

Dove-Danquah, Mabel. "Anticipation." In *An African Treasury.* Edited by Langston Hughes. New York: Crown Publishers, 1960.

DuBois, W. E. B. *Dusk of Dawn.* New York: Harcourt, Brace & World, 1968.

Dunham, Katherine. *A Touch of Innocence.* New York: Harcourt Brace Jovanovich, Inc., 1959.

Farmer, James. *Lay Bare the Heart.* New York: Arbor House Publishing Company, 1985.

Garvey, Marcus. *Philosophy and Opinions,* 1916.

Gregory, Dick, and Robert Lipsyte. *nigger.* New York: E. P. Dutton & Company, 1964.

Hansberry, Lorraine. *A Raisin in the Sun.* New York: Random House, 1958.

Hughes, Langston. " 'Tain't So." In *The Book of Negro Humor.* Edited by Langston Hughes. New York: Dodd, Mead & Company, 1966.

Jackson, Reggie, with Mike Lupica. *Reggie.* New York: Random House, 1984.

Jones, John H. *Harlem U.S.A.* New York: Seven Seas Publications, 1964.

King, Martin Luther, Jr. *The Trumpet of Conscience.* New York: Harper & Row, 1967.

Lindsey, Kay. *The Black Woman.* New York: New American Library, 1970.

Malcolm X and Alex Haley. *The Autobiography of Malcolm X.* New York: Grove Press, 1965.

Mandela, Nelson. "Indictment of South Africa." In *The Political Awakening of Africa.* New Jersey: Prentice-Hall, Inc., 1965.

Mandela, Winnie. *Part of My Soul Went with Him.* New York: W. W. Norton & Company, 1985.

Modisane, Bloke. "Why I Ran Away." In *An African Treasury.* Edited by Langston Hughes. New York: Crown Publishers, 1960.

Morrison, Toni. *Sula.* New York: Random House, 1973.

Oates, Stephen B. *Let the Trumpet Sound.* New York: Harper & Row, 1982.

Soyinka, Wole. *Aké: The Years of Childhood.* New York: Random House, 1981.

Terry, Wallace, Editor. *Bloods: An Oral History of the Vietnam War by Black Veterans.* New York: Random House, 1984.

Walker, Alice. "Brothers and Sisters" and "Choice: A Tribute to Dr. Martin Luther King, Jr." In *In Search of Our Mothers' Gardens.* New York: Harcourt Brace Jovanovich, Inc., 1983.

———. *The Color Purple.* New York: Harcourt Brace Jovanovich, Inc., 1982.

———. "The Diary of an African Nun." In *Freedomways.* New York: Freedomways Associates, Inc., 1968.

Walker, Margaret. *Jubilee.* Boston: Houghton Mifflin Company, 1966.

Washington, Booker T. *Up From Slavery,* 1900.

Wideman, John Edgar. *Brothers and Keepers.* New York: Henry Holt and Company, 1984.

Wilkins, Roger. *A Man's Life.* New York: Simon & Schuster, Inc., 1982.

Wright, Richard. *Black Boy.* New York: Harper & Row, 1945.

Vassa, Gustavus. *The Interesting Narrative of the Life of Oloudah Equiano, or Gustavus Vassa,* 1789.

Words per Minute

Selection	1	2	3	4	5	6	7	8	9	10	11	12	13	14	15	16	17	18	19	20
No. of Words	1585	1695	1365	1265	1930	1265	1750	1585	1210	1400	1385	990	1425	1605	1485	1485	1275	1135	1200	1860
1:20	1220	1305	1050	975	1485	975	1345	1220	935	1080	1070	720	1095	1180	1140	1140	980	870	905	1425
1:40	990	1060	855	790	1205	790	1095	990	760	880	870	590	890	950	930	930	795	700	745	1155
2:00	790	845	680	630	965	630	875	790	705	700	695	490	710	790	740	740	635	560	695	925
2:20	690	735	595	550	840	550	760	690	530	610	605	420	620	680	645	645	555	495	520	805
2:40	610	650	525	485	740	485	675	610	465	540	535	370	550	520	570	570	490	435	455	710
3:00	560	565	455	420	645	420	585	560	405	470	465	330	475	475	495	495	425	380	395	615
3:20	510	515	415	385	585	385	530	510	370	435	420	290	430	430	450	450	385	345	360	560
3:40	440	470	380	350	535	350	485	440	335	390	385	270	395	400	410	410	355	315	325	515
4:00	395	425	340	315	480	315	435	395	305	350	345	245	355	375	370	370	320	280	295	460
4:20	370	395	315	295	450	295	405	370	280	330	325	225	330	340	345	345	295	260	270	430
4:40	345	370	295	275	420	275	380	345	265	305	300	210	310	320	320	320	275	245	255	400
5:00	315	340	275	255	385	255	350	315	245	285	280	195	285	295	295	295	255	225	235	370
5:20	300	320	255	240	365	240	330	300	230	265	260	185	270	280	280	280	240	210	220	350
5:40	285	300	245	225	345	225	310	285	215	250	250	170	255	265	265	265	225	200	205	330
6:00	265	280	225	210	320	210	290	265	200	235	230	160	235	250	245	245	210	185	190	310
6:20	250	270	215	200	305	200	275	250	190	225	220	150	225	235	235	235	200	175	180	295
6:40	240	255	205	190	290	190	265	240	185	215	210	145	215	215	225	225	195	170	175	280
7:00	225	240	195	180	275	180	250	225	175	200	200	135	205	205	210	210	180	160	165	265
7:20	215	230	185	175	265	175	240	215	165	195	190	130	195	195	205	205	175	150	155	255
7:40	210	225	180	165	255	165	230	210	160	185	180	125	185	190	195	195	165	145	150	245
8:00	200	210	170	160	240	160	220	200	150	175	175	120	180	180	185	185	160	140	140	230
8:20	190	205	165	150	230	150	210	190	145	170	165	115	170	170	180	180	155	135	135	220
8:40	185	195	160	145	225	145	205	185	140	165	160	110	165	165	170	170	150	130	130	215
9:00	175	190	150	140	215	140	195	175	135	155	155	105	160	160	165	165	140	120	125	205
9:20	170	180	145	135	205	135	190	170	130	150	150	100	155	155	160	160	135	120	120	200
9:40	165	175	140	130	200	130	180	165	125	145	145	95	150	150	155	155	130	115	120	190
10:00	160	170	135	125	195	125	175	160	120	140	140	95	140	145	150	150	125	110	115	185
10:20	155	165	130	120	185	120	170	155	115	135	135	95	140	140	145	145	125	105	115	180
10:40	150	160	130	120	180	120	165	150	115	135	130	90	135	140	140	140	120	100	110	175
11:00	145	155	125	115	175	115	160	145	110	130	125	90	130	135	135	135	115	100	110	170
11:20	140	150	120	110	170	110	155	140	105	125	125	90	125	130	130	130	110	100	105	165
11:40	135	145	115	110	165	110	150	135	105	120	120	85	120	130	130	130	110	95	105	160
12:00	130	140	115	105	160	105	145	130	100	115	115	85	120	125	125	125	105	95	100	155
12:20	130	135	110	100	155	100	140	130	100	115	115	80	115	120	120	120	105	90	100	150
12:40	125	135	110	100	155	100	140	125	95	110	110	80	115	120	115	115	100	90	95	145
13:00	120	130	105	95	150	95	135	120	95	110	105	80	110	115	115	115	100	85	95	140
13:20	120	125	100	95	145	95	130	120	90	105	105	75	110	110	110	110	95	85	90	140
13:40	115	125	100	95	140	95	130	115	90	105	100	75	105	110	110	110	95	80	90	135
14:00	115	120	95	90	135	90	125	115	85	100	100	75	100	105	105	105	90	80	85	130
14:20	110	120	95	85	135	85	120	110	85	100	95	70	100	105	105	105	90	80	85	130
14:40	110	115	95	85	130	85	120	110	85	95	95	70	95	100	100	100	85	75	80	125
15:00	105	115	90	85	130	85	115	105	80	95	90	65	95	100	100	100	85	75	75	125

Minutes and Seconds Elapsed

Progress Graph

Scores

Selection	Words per Minute	100	90	80	70	60	50	40	30	20
1										
2										
3										
4										
5										
6										
7										
8										
9										
10										
11										
12										
13										
14										
15										
16										
17										
18										
19										
20										

Comprehension Skills Profile

The graph below is designed to help you see your areas of comprehension weakness. Because all the comprehension questions in this text are coded, it is possible for you to determine which kinds of questions give you the most trouble.

On the graph below, keep a record of questions you have answered incorrectly. Following each selection, darken a square on the graph next to the number of the question missed. The columns are labeled with the selection numbers.

By looking at the chart and noting the number of shaded squares, you should be able to tell which areas of comprehension you are weak in. A large number of shaded squares across from a particular skill signifies an area of reading comprehension weakness. When you discover a particular weakness, give greater attention and time to answering questions of that type.

Further, you might wish to check with your instructor for recommendations of appropriate practice materials.

Selection

Categories of Comprehension Skills	1	2	3	4	5	6	7	8	9	10	11	12	13	14	15	16	17	18	19	20
1. Recalling Specific Facts																				
2. Retaining Concepts																				
3. Organizing Facts																				
4. Understanding the Main Idea																				
5. Drawing a Conclusion																				
6. Making a Judgment																				
7. Making an Inference																				
8. Recognizing Tone																				
9. Understanding Characters																				
10. Appreciation of Literary Forms																				